# voices of the truewoman movement

# voices of the truewoman movement

## A Call to the Counter-Revolution

## NANCY LEIGH DeMOSS

Including contributions by
**John Piper**
**Joni Eareckson Tada**
**Janet Parshall**
**Mary Kassian**

MOODY PUBLISHERS

CHICAGO

All Scripture quotations, unless otherwise indicated, are taken from *The Holy Bible, English Standard Version.* Copyright © 2000; 2001 by Crossway Bibles, a division of Good News Publishers. Used by permission. All rights reserved.

Scripture quotations marked NKJV are taken from *The New King James Version.* Copyright © 1982 Thomas Nelson, Inc. Used by permission. All rights reserved.

Scripture quotations marked NIV are taken from the Holy Bible, New International Version®, NIV®. Copyright © 1973, 1978, 1984 by Biblica, Inc.™ Used by permission of Zondervan. All rights reserved worldwide.

Scripture quotations marked KJV are taken from the King James Version.

Scripture quotations marked NASB are taken from the New American Standard Bible®, Copyright © 1960, 1962, 1963, 1968, 1971, 1972, 1973, 1975, 1977, 1995 by The Lockman Foundation. Used by permission. (www.Lockman.org)

Emphasis in Scripture quotations are the authors.'

Editor: Betsey Newenhuyse
Cover design: FaceOut Studio—formerly The DesignWorks Group, Inc.
Interior design: Smartt Guys design

**Library of Congress Cataloging-in-Publication Data**

DeMoss, Nancy Leigh.
Voices of the true woman movement : a call to the counter-revolution /
Nancy Leigh DeMoss ; including contributions by John Piper ... [et al.].
    p. cm.
  Includes bibliographical references and index.
  ISBN 978-0-8024-1286-7
  1. Christian women--Religious life. 2. Women--Religious
aspects--Christianity. I. Piper, John, 1946- II. Title.
BV4527.D4625 2010
248.8'43--dc22
                    2009053551

We hope you enjoy this book from Moody Publishers. Our goal is to provide high-quality, thought-provoking books and products that connect truth to your real needs and challenges. For more information on other books and products written and produced from a biblical perspective, go to www.moodypublishers.com or write to:

Moody Publishers
820 N. LaSalle Boulevard
Chicago, IL 60610

1 3 5 7 9 10 8 6 4 2

*Printed in the United States of America*

## Now is the time . . .

*Today, more than ever, I believe that **now is the time** for "true women" to . . .*
- *Discover and embrace God's created design and mission for their lives*
  - *Reflect the beauty and heart of Christ to our world*
- *Be intentional about passing the baton of Truth on to the next generation*
  - *Pray earnestly for an outpouring of God's Spirit in our families, churches, nation, and world*

—NANCY LEIGH DEMOSS

*The **time is ripe** for a new movement—a seismic, holy quake of countercultural Christian women who dare to take God at His Word, who have the courage to stand against the popular tide, choosing to believe and delight in God's plan for male and female.*

—MARY KASSIAN

*It **is time** for women of biblical faith to reclaim our territory. We know the Designer. We have His instruction manual. If we don't display the Divine design of His female creation, no one will. But if we do, it will be a profound testimony to a watching, needy world.[1]*

—SUSAN HUNT

*Who knows whether you have come to the kingdom **for such a time** as this?*

—ESTHER 4:14 NKJV

# Contents

# Contributors

**Pastor John Piper** has been married to Noël for more than forty years. They have five children and ten grandchildren. Dr. Piper is the author of over thirty books and is Pastor for Preaching and Vision at Bethlehem Baptist Church in Minneapolis, Minnesota. (www.desiringgod.org)

**Nancy Leigh DeMoss** is a mentor and "spiritual mother" to hundreds of thousands of women who have read her best-selling books and who listen to her two daily radio programs, *Revive Our Hearts* and *Seeking Him*. (www.reviveourhearts.com)

**Mary Kassian** and her husband, Brent, who make their home in Canada, are celebrating nearly thirty years of marriage and have three young adult sons and one daughter-in-law. Mary is a distinguished professor of Women's Studies at Southern Baptist Theological Seminary in Louisville, Kentucky, and is the author of several books including *The Feminist Mistake* and *Girls Gone Wise in a World Gone Wild*. (www.girlsgonewise.com)

**Janet Parshall** and her attorney husband, Craig, have been married for nearly forty years. They have four adult children and six grandchildren. Her years as a stay-at-home mom prepared her for her current role as the host of two nationally syndicated radio shows: *Janet Parshall's America* and the weekend program *Talking it Over With Janet Parshall* on the Moody Radio Network. (www.jpamerica.com)

**Karen Loritts** enjoys her four grown children and seven grandchildren. A speaker, teacher, and author, she has served in ministry since 1972 with her husband, Crawford, who is currently the senior pastor at Fellowship Bible Church in Roswell, Georgia.

**Joni Eareckson Tada** is the Founder and CEO of *Joni and Friends*, an organization that promotes Christian ministry in the disability community. Ken Tada, Joni's best friend and her husband of nearly thirty years, serves with her as the director of ministry development. (www.joniandfriends.org)

**Fern Nichols** and her husband, Rle, have been married for over forty years. Their four children were the inspiration for her to found *Moms In Touch International*, a ministry that has mobilized tens of thousands of moms in over 130 countries to pray for their children and schools. (www. momsintouch.org)

# Introduction

One of the great challenges in our day is the vast number of voices vying for our attention.

The roar of our culture and those who speak for it is inescapable and deafening. Voices speak to us persistently, incessantly—from the big screen, our flat screen TVs, our laptop screens, and our smartphone screens. Add to that the surround-sound voices of friends, family members, and acquaintances, along with the nagging voices of our past, our failures, and our fears, and the never-ending chatter of our own thoughts.

So much is determined by which voices we hear and heed: our sense of who we are and why we are here; the way we relate to others; the choices we make; the way we spend our moments and years; our personal, emotional, and spiritual well-being; and yes, the ultimate outcome of our lives.

Conflicting voices were an issue all the way back in the garden of Eden. The voice of God: *"You are free to eat from every tree but one—if you eat from that tree, you will die."* The voice of the Serpent: *"You won't die—in fact, you'll become like God!"* Which to listen to?

Eve was led astray by listening to the wrong voice. And she proceeded to become a voice that echoed the deception of the Serpent himself as she influenced her husband to choose to reject the voice of God.

God to Adam:

*Because you have listened to the voice of your wife*
*and have eaten of the tree*
*of which I commanded you,*
*"You shall not eat of it,"*
*cursed is the ground because of you;*
*in pain you shall eat of it all the days of your life.* (Genesis 3:17)

I don't think it would be overstating the case to say that most if not all of the pain, dysfunction, and distress we experience in this broken world comes as a result of listening to voices that counter rather than affirm the voice of God.

Since the 1950s, a powerful chorus of voices has called out in unison to women—urging us to partake of the fruit of independence, self-reliance, and self-determination. "Have it your way," they chant. "You deserve a break today." "It's all about you."

Slick advertising and packaging have made the world's offer, like the forbidden fruit in the garden, appear to be "good . . . a delight to the eyes . . . desired to make one wise" (Genesis 3:6).

These voices are "loud" and "seductive." Madame Folly and her companions call out "to those who pass by, who are going straight on their way," to the one "who lacks sense" (cf. Proverbs 9:13–18).

These voices can be heard everywhere in our culture—in best-selling books, popular magazines, award-winning movies, Top Ten hit songs, and daytime, primetime, and late night TV. As multiple generations of women have now responded en masse to the siren call, there has been a sea change in our world, a revolution of Copernican proportions.

Many are quick to point to the gains women enjoy today as a result of this revolution. However, they are not so quick to recognize the enormous losses and pain that I believe more than offset those gains.

In the course of ministering to women for more than thirty years, I have witnessed firsthand the fall-out of listening to the wrong voices. I have seen it in the thousands of e-mails and letters our ministry has received from women whose hearts and hopes have been shattered. I have seen it in the eyes of women who are experiencing the disorientation and damage that result when the din of this world's voices drowns out the one Voice we most need to hear.

*The voice of the Lord is powerful;*
*The voice of the Lord is full of majesty.* (Psalm 29:4)

His is the voice of Wisdom—full of grace and truth.

When the voice of man's wisdom echoed from the mountaintop, *"a cloud overshadowed them, and a voice came out of the cloud, 'This is my beloved Son; listen to him'"* (Mark 9:7).

Years ago, the Lord began to lay on my heart a burden for a new women's movement—a counter-cultural revolution, in which women would reject the seductive voices of this world and would incline their hearts to listen to Christ and follow His voice.

*Revive Our Hearts* was birthed out of that burden. We have sought to faithfully proclaim the Word of God to women and to point them to Christ, so that they might hear His voice penetrating the clouds and confusion of the world's voices.

In October 2008 over six thousand women from forty-eight states and seven countries gathered in Chicago for the first True Woman conference, hosted by *Revive Our Hearts*, along with our ministry partners Moody Bible Institute, FamilyLife, Moms in Touch, and Life Action Ministries. These women came together to hear God's Word and to affirm His mission and purpose for their lives.

I was joined on the platform by others who share my concern for women and who are committed to proclaim His Word rather than their own. Beginning with Pastor John Piper in the opening session, these speakers united their voices in calling women to be "true women" of God, to anchor their lives in His Word, to live out what it means to be redeemed women, and to embrace His calling for their lives.

Thousands of women who heard the message that weekend in the Schaumburg Convention Center and by means of a live video stream, have taken it to heart; they have added their voices to the chorus and are continuing to sound it forth in their churches and communities across the United States and around the world.

This volume is a collection of the messages that were presented in the plenary sessions at True Woman '08. It is not intended to be a comprehensive treatment of biblical womanhood. But these messages represent the heart and voices of the True Woman movement. This is a movement based on and submitted to the authority of the Word of God. A movement of women seeking fulfillment, not in personal accomplishment, but in the person of the Lord Jesus Christ. Women who are living for something and Someone greater than themselves. Women who recognize how far we've moved from God's purposes and ideal and are seeking to answer His call to biblical womanhood. Women who believe that true freedom is found in the whole-hearted and joyous expression of who God created us to be.

Regardless of where you find yourself in the stream of this movement—whether already deeply immersed in it, just testing the waters, or perhaps even a skeptic or detractor—as you read these pages, I pray that your heart will be tuned to hear His voice and that you will be drawn into a deeper level of love for Christ and trust in His Word.

One final thought: It is extremely difficult, if not impossible, to live out our calling as women of God, on our own. I have been greatly helped and encouraged in my journey by keeping company with other women (including those who contributed to this book) who share my desire to be "true women" and to make the gospel believable in our world. To help you cultivate those kinds of relationships, we've included a study guide at the end of this book ("Going Deeper"), designed to facilitate discussion of each chapter. So rather than just reading this book on your own, why not ask a friend—or several—to join you. And be sure to check out www .TrueWoman.com for practical ideas on how to be a part of this counter-cultural movement—a woman who reflects the beauty and wonder of Christ to our generation and the next!

My hope and that of the other voices represented in this book is that you will join thousands of other women who are saying "*Yes, Lord,* I want to be Your true woman," and that you will become one more voice of the True Woman movement—sounding forth His Word and His grace in your sphere of influence—"for such a time as this"!

— *Nancy Leigh DeMoss*

PART ONE

# foundations of
# true womanhood

*In order to learn what it means to be a woman, we must start*
*with the One who made her.*[1]

— ELISABETH ELLIOT

# the ultimate meaning of
# true womanhood

## JOHN PIPER

My aim in this message is to clarify from God's Word the ultimate meaning of true womanhood, and to motivate you, by God's grace, to embrace it as your highest calling. What I will say is foundational to the "True Woman Manifesto" which I regard as a faithful, clear, true, and wise document.

I would like to begin by stating one huge assumption that I bring to this chapter. I mention it partly because it may give you an emotional sense of what I hope you become. And I mention it partly because it explains why I minister the way I do and why this message sounds the way it does.

My assumption is that *wimpy theology makes wimpy women*. And I don't like wimpy women. I didn't marry a wimpy woman. And with Noël, I am trying to raise my teenage daughter Talitha not to be a wimpy woman.

### Marie Durant

The opposite of a wimpy woman is not a brash, pushy, loud, controlling, sassy, uppity, arrogant Amazon. The opposite of a wimpy woman is fourteen-year-old Marie Durant, a French Christian in the seventeenth century who was arrested for being a Protestant and told she could be released if she said one phrase: "I abjure." Instead, she wrote on the wall of her cell, "Resist," and stayed there thirty-eight years until she died, doing just that.[1]

## Gladys and Esther Staines

The opposite of a wimpy woman is Gladys Staines who in 1999, after serving with her husband Graham in India for three decades learned that he and their two sons, Phillip (10) and Timothy (6), had been set on fire and burned alive by the very people they had served for thirty-four years, said, "I have only one message for the people of India. I'm not bitter. Neither am I angry. Let us burn hatred and spread the flame of Christ's love."

The opposite of a wimpy woman is her thirteen-year-old daughter Esther (rightly named!) who said, when asked how she felt about her father's murder, "I praise the Lord that He found my father worthy to die for Him."[2]

## Krista and Vicki

The opposite of a wimpy woman is Krista and Vicki, friends of ours in Minneapolis, who between them have had over sixty-five surgeries because of so-called birth defects, Apert Syndrome and Hypertelorism, and who testify today through huge challenges, "I praise You because I am fearfully and wonderfully made; Your works are wonderful, I know that full well"; and this: "Even though my life has been difficult, I know that God loves me and created me just the way I am. He has taught me to persevere and to trust Him more than anything."

## Joni Eareckson Tada

The opposite of a wimpy woman is Joni Eareckson Tada, who has spent the last forty-one years in a wheelchair, and prays, "Oh, thank you, thank you for this wheelchair! By tasting hell in this life, I've been driven to think seriously about what faces me in the next. This paralysis is my greatest mercy."[3]

## Suzie

The opposite of a wimpy woman is Suzie, who lost her husband four years ago at age fifty-nine, found breast cancer three months later, then lost her mom and writes, "Now I see that I have been crying for the wrong kind of help. I now see that my worst suffering is my sin—my sin of self-centeredness and self-pity. . . . I know that with His grace, His lovingkindness, and His merciful help, my thoughts can be reformed and my life conformed to be more like His Son."

## Wimpy Theology Makes Wimpy Women

Wimpy theology makes wimpy women. That's my assumption that I bring to this chapter. Wimpy theology simply does not give a woman a God that is big enough, strong enough, wise enough, and good enough to handle the realities of life in a way that magnifies the infinite worth of Jesus Christ.

Wimpy theology is plagued by woman-centeredness and man-centeredness. Wimpy theology doesn't have the granite foundation of God's sovereignty or the solid steel structure of a great God-centered purpose for all things.

> *Wimpy theology does not give a woman a God that is big enough.*

## The Ultimate Purpose for the Universe

So I turn to my main point, the ultimate meaning of true womanhood, and start by stating this great God-centered purpose of all things:

God's ultimate purpose for the universe and for all of history and for your life is to display the glory of Christ in its highest expression, namely, in His dying to make a rebellious people His everlasting and supremely happy bride.

To say it another way, God's ultimate purpose in creating the world and choosing to let it become the sin-wracked world that it is, is so that the greatness of the glory of Christ could be put on display at Calvary where

He bought His rebellious bride at the cost of His life.

I base this statement of God's ultimate purpose on several texts. For example, Revelation 13:8 where John refers to God writing names "before the foundation of the world in the book of life of the Lamb who was slain." So in God's mind Christ was already slain before the creation of the world. This was His plan from the beginning. Why?

Because in being slain "to make a wretch His treasure"—to make a rebel His bride—the glory of His grace would shine most brightly, and that was His ultimate purpose according to Ephesians 1:4–6, "In love he predestined us for adoption as sons through Jesus Christ . . . *to the praise of the glory of his grace.*"

## The Glory of Christ at the Cross

From the very beginning, God's design in creating the universe and governing it the way He does has been to put the glory of His grace on display in the death of His Son for the sake of His bride. "Husbands, love your wives, *as Christ loved the church and gave himself up for her,* that he might sanctify her . . . that he might present the church to himself in splendor, without spot or wrinkle or any such thing, that she might be holy and without blemish" (Ephesians 5:25–27). The ultimate purpose of creation and redemption is to put the glory of Christ on display in purchasing and purifying His bride, the church.

## True Womanhood: At the Center of God's Purpose

Now where does this take us in regard to the ultimate meaning of true womanhood? It does not take us to wimpy theology or wimpy women. It is not wimpy to say that God created the universe and governs all things to magnify His own grace in the death of His Son for the salvation of His bride. That's not wimpy. And it doesn't lead to wimpy womanhood.

But it does lead to womanhood. True womanhood. In fact, it leads to the mind-boggling truth that womanhood and manhood— femininity and masculinity—belong at the center of God's ultimate purpose. Womanhood and manhood were not an afterthought or a peripheral thought in God's plan. God designed them precisely so that they would serve to display the glory of His Son dying to have His happy, admiring bride.

## Created to Display Jesus' Glory

Genesis 1:27 says, "God created man in his own image, in the image of God he created him; male and female he created them." Sometimes we make the mistake of thinking God created us this way, and then later when Christ came to do His saving work, God looked around and said, "Well, that's a good analogy, man and woman. I'll describe My Son's salvation with that. I'll say it's like a husband dying to save his bride."

> *He created us as male and female precisely so that we could display the glory of His Son.*

It didn't happen like that. God did not look around and *find* manhood and womanhood to be a helpful comparison to His Son's relation to the church. He *created* us as male and female precisely so that we could display the glory of His Son. Our sexuality is designed for the glory of the Son of God—especially the glory of His dying to have His admiring bride.

In Ephesians 5:31, Paul quotes Genesis 2:24, "Therefore a man shall leave his father and mother and hold fast to his wife, and the two shall become one flesh." And then he adds this, "This mystery is profound, and I am saying that it refers to Christ and the church." In other words, from the beginning, manhood and womanhood were designed to display the glory of Christ in His relationship to the church, His bride.

## A Distinctive Calling to Display the Glory of Christ

In other words, the ultimate meaning of true womanhood is this: It is a distinctive calling of God to display the glory of His Son in ways that would not be displayed if there were no womanhood. If there were only generic persons and not male and female, the glory of Christ would be diminished in the world. When God described the glorious work of His Son as the sacrifice of a husband for His bride, He was telling us why He made us male and female. He made us this way so that our maleness and femaleness would display more fully the glory of His Son in relation to His blood-bought bride.

This means that if you try to reduce womanhood to physical features and biological functions, and then determine your role in the world merely on the basis of competencies, you don't just miss the point of womanhood, you diminish the glory of Christ in your own life. True womanhood is indispensable in God's purpose to display the fullness of the glory of His Son. Your distinctive female personhood is not incidental. It exists because of its God-designed relationship to the central event of history, the death of the Son of God.

So let me say a word about what that looks like if you are married and if you are single.

## A Word to the Married

First, a word to the married. Paul says in Ephesians 5:22–24, "Wives, submit to your own husbands, as to the Lord. For the husband is the head of the wife even as Christ is the head of the church, his body, and is himself its Savior. Now as the church submits to Christ, so also wives should submit in everything to their husbands."

The point here is that marriage is meant to display the covenant-keeping love between Christ and His church. And the way it does this is by men being men and women being women in marriage. These are no more interchangeable than Christ is interchangeable with the church. Men take their cues from Christ as the head, and women take their cues from what the church is called to be in her allegiance to Christ. This is described by Paul in terms of headship and submission. Here are my definitions of headship and submission based on this text:

• *Headship* is the divine calling of a husband to take primary responsibility for Christ-like, servant leadership, protection, and provision in the home.

• *Submission* is the divine calling of a wife to honor and affirm her husband's leadership and help carry it through according to her gifts.

The point here is not to go into detail about how this gets worked out from marriage to marriage. The point is that these two, headship and submission, are different. They correspond to true manhood and true womanhood, which are different. And these differences are absolutely essential by God's design, so that marriage will display, as in a mirror dimly, something of the glory of the sacrificial love of Christ for His bride and the lavish reverence and admiration of the bride for her husband.

I know this leaves a hundred questions unanswered—about unbelieving husbands, and believing husbands who don't take spiritual leadership, and wives who resist their husbands' leadership, and those who receive it but don't affirm it. But if you—you married women—embrace the truth that your womanhood, true womanhood, is uniquely and indispensably created by God to display the glory of His Son in the way you relate to your husband, you will have a calling of infinite significance.

But what if you aren't married?

## A Word to Singles

The apostle Paul clearly loved his singleness because of the radical freedom for ministry that it gave him (1 Corinthians 7:32–38). One of the reasons he was free to celebrate his singleness and call others to join him in it, is that, even though marriage is meant to display the glory of Christ, there are truths about Christ and His kingdom that shine more clearly through singleness than through marriage. I'll give you three examples:

1) *A life of Christ-exalting singleness bears witness that the family of God grows not by propagation through sexual intercourse, but by regeneration through faith in Christ.* If you never marry, and if you embrace a lifetime of chastity and biological childlessness, and if you receive this from the Lord's hand as a gift with contentment, and if you gather to yourself the needy and the lonely, and spend yourself for the gospel without

self-pity, because Christ has met your need, then He will be mightily glorified in your life, and particularly so because you are a woman.

2) *A life of Christ-exalting singleness bears witness that relationships in Christ are more permanent, and more precious, than relationships in families.* The single woman who turns away from regretting the absence of her own family, and gives herself to creating God's family in the church, will find the flowering of her womanhood in ways she never dreamed, and Christ will be uniquely honored because of it.

3) *A life of Christ-exalting singleness bears witness that marriage is temporary, and finally gives way to the relationship to which it was pointing all along: Christ and the church*—the way a picture is no longer needed when you see face-to-face. Marriage is a beautiful thing. But it is not the main thing. If it were, Jesus would not have said, "In the resurrection they neither marry nor are given in marriage, but are like angels in heaven" (Matthew 22:30). Single womanhood, content to walk with Christ, is a great witness that He is a better husband than any man, and in the end, will be the only husband in the universe.

In other words, true womanhood can flourish in marriage and singleness.

## True Womanhood for the Glory of Christ

I commend to you this truth: The ultimate purpose of God in history is the display of the glory of His Son in dying for His bride. God has created man as male and female because there are aspects of Christ's glory which would not be known if they were not reflected in the complementary differences of manhood and womanhood. Therefore, true womanhood is a distinctive calling of God to display the glory of His Son in ways that would not be displayed if there were no womanhood.

Married womanhood has its unique potential for magnifying Christ that single womanhood does not have. Single womanhood has its unique potential for magnifying Christ which married womanhood does not have.

So whether you marry or remain single, do not settle for a wimpy theology. It is beneath you. God is too great. Christ is too glorious. True womanhood is too strategic. Don't waste it. Your womanhood—your true womanhood—was made for the glory of Jesus Christ.

# from Him, through Him,
# **to Him**

## **NANCY LEIGH DeMOSS**

On a recent trip to Colorado, I joined some adventurous friends on a day-long "jeeping" excursion in the Rocky Mountains. It was an unforgettable experience. Maneuvering around one hairpin curve after another, we made our way higher and higher up (and later back down) the narrow, sometimes treacherous, mountain trails. At times, we found ourselves perilously close to the edge, peering down the side of the mountain, wondering how much further we had to climb to make it to the peak. We got out and hiked at points, our breathing increasingly labored in the thin air, watching our steps ever so carefully, so as not to lose our footing on the steep trails.

When we finally reached the summit, towering over 13,000 feet, our effort was rewarded, as we climbed out of our vehicle and looked down and around at the breathtaking view that surrounded us on every side. We were awestruck by the beauty, the magnificence, the handiwork of God on full display.

That memorable moment comes to mind when I read a passage of Scripture I'd like us to consider together—a passage that I believe is at the heart of the True Woman movement:

*Oh, the depth of the riches and wisdom and knowledge of God! How unsearchable are his judgments and how inscrutable his ways! "For who has known the mind of the Lord, or who has been his counselor?" "Or who has given a gift to him that he might be repaid?" For from him and through him and to Him are all things. To him be glory forever. Amen.* (Romans 11:33–36)

When the apostle Paul wrote these words to the church in Rome, I believe he was experiencing a sense much like what we felt at the top of that Rocky Mountain pass. Let me give you some context. In the first eleven chapters of Romans, Paul lays out the basic doctrines of our faith—the sinfulness of man, the amazing grace of God, the salvation that is possible for us through Jesus Christ. Then, in the remainder of the book—chapters 12 through 16—Paul makes practical application of everything he has written before. If the first eleven chapters are the "what" of the gospel, the last part of Romans is the "*so* what"—how are we to live in light of these great truths? And the doxology of Romans 11:33–36 serves as a bridge between the two.

Just prior to these words, in chapters 9–11 (a section of Scripture that's admittedly difficult to understand and one many are prone to skip over), Paul explores the mysteries of God's sovereign, electing grace, God's plan for redeeming both Jews and Gentiles. He talks about Israel's past, present, and future role in God's great redemptive story. He explains how in God's sovereignty, the Jews' rejection of Christ is actually the means by which Gentiles have come to accept Him as Savior. Then he writes about how in God's great mercy He will yet fulfill His plan for Israel in spite of their rejection.

I'm oversimplifying to try summarizing such magnificent doctrines in a single paragraph, but even in the space of a few sentences, we clearly see that this divine plan is not the way we would have scripted the story. God has designed history in such a way that even human unbelief and rebellion cannot thwart His final, eternal purposes. And I'm sure as Paul, under the inspiration of the Holy Spirit, began scratching out these words and concepts in written form, he—like we—was left to scratch his head and ask the Lord, "How did You come up with this?"

So in a trek not unlike our Jeep ride in the Colorado mountains, in the first eleven chapters of his epistle to the Romans, Paul scales higher and higher through the astounding mysteries of God, weaving his way through one difficult passage after another. At the end of chapter eleven he finally reaches the summit, where he can look back down over the path he has taken. He pauses to take in the awesome view beneath and around him: the sovereignty of God, His electing mercy and grace, His eternal plan for the ages.

And as Paul pauses to contemplate it all, he is suddenly struck speechless. Words fail to explain the view, just as there are no adequate words to capture the snow-streaked, aspen-lined glories of God's western American mountainscape from thousands of feet above the surface. I can still see it, but I can't quite describe it. And Paul, sensing all of this and infinitely more, breaks out into a hymn of praise, like crashing cymbals in the finale of a symphonic masterpiece.

> *Oh, the depth . . . how unsearchable . . . how inscrutable . . . to Him be glory forever.*

## Deeper Still

This paragraph in Romans may seem like an odd place to launch into a discussion on true womanhood. At first glance, it may not appear to have much to do with the subject. However, as I have meditated on Paul's words, I have been reminded that they are foundational to what it means to be a true woman of God and to everything my sisters will address in the chapters that follow.

This passage provides a framework and context for our lives as women. It gives us a fixed reference point for our hearts. It tethers us to God's ultimate, eternal purposes. It gives us a perspective—a grid—for responding to His sovereign choices in our lives, especially those we cannot understand or explain.

And it all starts here: *"Oh, the depth . . ."*

The Greek word translated "depth" in our Bibles is similar to our English word "bath." The way we sink down into hot water in a bathtub—until we're submerged from neck to toe—the depths of God's "riches and wisdom and knowledge" overwhelm us. They rise above us. They roll beneath us. They float all around us. We just want to bathe in them.

> *But though we can never reach the bottom of God's unfathomable ways, we do know what it's like to reach the bottom of our own strength.*

On January 23, 1960, a U.S. Navy lieutenant and a Swiss scientist took a deep-diving, submersible vessel known as a bathyscaphe down to the deepest spot on earth—the Marianas Trench, a chasm in the Pacific near the island of Guam. Seven miles straight down under the ocean's surface—35,800 feet—a massive, record-setting human feat. It took them nearly five hours, but they were finally able to locate the bottom of the ocean floor. Once there, you can go no farther.

This is not the case, however, with the depths of God. Five hours, five years, five whole lifetimes would not be enough to plumb the depths of His riches, wisdom, and knowledge. Try as you might, you can't get your mind around them. He is inexhaustible, limitless, immeasurable. *"Oh, the depth . . ."*

But though we can never reach the bottom of God's unfathomable ways, we do know what it's like to reach the bottom of our own strength. Perhaps you've been there—perhaps you *are* there—down where life drags the floor of all human abilities, where everything feels hopeless and pointless and impossible to handle. This is where many women give up and call it quits, or slink away into a pit of bitterness, or turn their frustrations on those nearest them—*anything* to cope with life at the bottom. But the true woman knows that deeper than her own limitations and problems, is the bedrock of God's riches, wisdom, and knowledge. His unseen yet sovereign, eternal purposes are underneath it all, holding it all together.

It reminds me of the well-known account from Corrie ten Boom's life, when her sister Betsie, wasting away and dying in the Nazi concentration camp at Ravensbruck, urged her to "tell people what we have learned here . . . that there is no pit so deep that He is not deeper still."

This became the theme of Corrie's ministry for the rest of her life. Miraculously released from the horrible conditions that had claimed her sister's life, Corrie traveled the world into her eighties, declaring the depths of the riches and wisdom and knowledge and love of God. "They will listen to us, Corrie," Betsie had told her. "They will listen to us because we have been here."

Your problems may be deeper than ever. Your issues and challenges may never before have reached such depths as you're experiencing now. But no matter how low they've taken you, there is something—Someone—who is deeper still. "The eternal God is your dwelling place, and underneath are the everlasting arms" (Deuteronomy 33:27).

### *"Oh, the depth of the riches . . . of God"*

Deep inside the earth are vast riches still waiting to be found. Some estimate that six billion dollars' worth of sunken treasure lies undiscovered, scattered across the darkened ocean depths of the globe.

The world's deepest gold mine, located near Johannesburg, South Africa, extends two full miles into the earth, having produced more than a hundred million ounces—three thousand tons—of pure gold since it began operations in the early 1950s. Once described as the eighth wonder of the world, the Driefontein mine employs nearly 17,000 people who spend all day every day gathering gold from the earth. And still there's more—this one mine is expected to produce at least a million ounces a year, for the next twenty years.[1]

But God's riches go deeper still.

Earlier in the book of Romans, Paul talks about the "riches of his kindness and forbearance and patience" (Romans 2:4), as well as "the riches of his glory" (9:23). In Ephesians he declares God to be "rich in mercy" (Ephesians 2:4), extolling the "riches of his grace, which he lavished upon us, in all wisdom and insight" (1:7–8). But unlike the riches on the ocean's floor,

> *God will never experience economic collapse or even the slightest wave or bobble of uncertainty.*

which could eventually be collected if a way were available to reach them— unlike the riches of a gold mine, which eventually yields all the precious metal it contains—the gold in God's mine will never be emptied. Never. It is limitless. It is inexhaustible.

God will never experience economic collapse or even the slightest wave or bobble of uncertainty. When the Scripture addresses our human lacks and shortages, the promise is that "God will supply every need of yours according to his riches in glory in Christ Jesus" (Philippians 4:19). His always-available provision for your needs will neither strain nor drain the budget of the Most High. Rather, it will continue pouring from His hand into your life, utterly free and fathomless, from His bottomless resources.

Whatever your need, whatever your deficit, the riches of God are more than what's required.

### *"Oh, the depth . . . of the wisdom and knowledge of God"*

God knows everything—and everything *about* everything! Everything about the world, everything about history, everything about the future, everything about elections, everything about our economy and where it's headed. And not only does He know all things from a comprehensive, macro perspective, He also knows everything in miniature, down to the tiniest detail. God has complete wisdom and knowledge; He knows everything about your life.

- He knows everything about your past, your present, and your future.
- He knows the things you've done and the things that have been done to you.
- He knows things you've never told a single soul.

- He knows all about your family situation.
- He knows all about your financial needs.
- He knows all about your physical challenges.
- He knows all about your motives.
- He knows all about your sins.
- He knows all about your fears and insecurities.

He knows all of mine too. He knows it all. He knows everything.

The wisdom and knowledge of God are infinitely greater than our own. The human mind could never have come up with a way that sinners could be justified and declared righteous before a holy God. No one has wisdom and knowledge like that. But the wisdom of God devised a way—before sin had even entered the world!

And regardless of how complex, convoluted, or impossible your situation may seem or actually be right now, the wisdom of God is much more than adequate to walk you through it. "For the foolishness of God is wiser than men, and the weakness of God is stronger than men" (1 Corinthians 1:25).

*"Oh, the depth of the riches and wisdom and knowledge of God!"*

## Beyond Knowing

*"How unsearchable are his judgments and how inscrutable his ways."* I like J. B. Phillips's paraphrase of this verse: "How could man ever understand his reasons for action, or explain his methods of working?" Or as the King James Version puts it, His ways are "past finding out." His decrees and decisions are "unsearchable"—they are beyond our human capacity to fathom.

"Inscrutable" is not a word we toss around in everyday conversation. Define.com defines it this way: "incapable of being searched into and understood by inquiry or study; impossible or difficult to be explained or accounted for satisfactorily; incomprehensible; not easily understood; mysterious."

In other words, no matter how brilliant a person may be, no matter how hard or long she works at it, she can never completely understand why (or how) God does what He does. It's unknowable, unsearchable, inscrutable. That's how Paul describes God's judgments and His ways.

Try doing a Google search on the "judgments of God," and you'll get 313,000 hits. Search the "ways of God," and you'll discover a million more. But even if you could take the time to investigate every one of these sites and all the various trails they could take you to, you'd barely have skimmed the surface of the depths of His ways. We simply cannot know all that He is doing or why He does what He does. Those answers are hidden, locked away in the mind of God, and we have no choice but to leave them there. In fact, rather than demanding answers to our questions, we should trust that He knows what we need to know—as well as what we don't—and that it is His kindness that withholds from us what would be too grand or painful for us to absorb in our mortal minds.

> *"In every situation and circumstance of your life, God is always doing a thousand different things that you cannot see and you do not know."*

Years ago, I heard Pastor John Piper make a statement that resonated deeply in my heart. I've shared it with many others since then in various settings. He said, *"In every situation and circumstance of your life, God is always doing a thousand different things that you cannot see and you do not know."* Though at times God reveals some portion of His will clearly to us, enough that we can detect a *few* things He is doing and say, "Oh, that makes sense," the vast majority of His work is behind the scenes, providentially obscured from our view.

I repeated this statement of Pastor Piper's recently while talking with a mom whose daughter has chosen a prodigal lifestyle. She looked back at me through tears, even as her face showed visible signs of relief. She said, "I need that quote hanging in my home where I can look at it all the time." Yes, and all of us need it hanging in our hearts. God is at work. You may not see it. But you know it's true.

### *"How unsearchable..."*

You will never be able to fully explore what God is doing in your life. You cannot possibly see the end or the outcome... not yet anyway. You cannot fathom the means He has devised to fulfill His holy purposes through you. He doesn't owe you an explanation. He is God, and He is working.

### *"How inscrutable..."*

Our inability to fathom God's ways led Paul from exclamatory statements to three rhetorical questions found in Romans 11 verses 34 and 35, each with the same answer: "For who has known the mind of the Lord?" Answer? *No one.* "Or who has been his counselor?" *No one.* "Or who has given a gift to him that he might be repaid?" *No one. No one.* A thousand times... *no one.*

How many times have you tried to tell God what He should do in a certain situation? How many times have you questioned whether He knows what He's doing? How many times have you felt like He owed you something for all you've invested in trying to live for Him?

Job knew the feeling... and got this answer in response, amid several chapters' worth of Leviathan sightings and such: "Who has first given to me, that I should repay him? Whatever is under the whole heaven is mine" (Job 41:11).

Oh, dear sister, if we could just lay hold of this in our hearts. God doesn't need to consult with anyone about anything. He never needs input or counsel, needs no guidance or advice—not from me, not from you, not from anyone. He possesses limitless wisdom. He never needs to call a hotline, use a lifeline, or phone directory assistance for information. He is altogether self-sufficient and independent. He never needs assistance from anything or anyone outside of Himself.

How just the opposite we are—utterly, totally, absolutely dependent on Him. He doesn't need us—we need Him! Even the seemingly simple task of drawing a single breath—in and out, just one time—requires lung capacity and involuntary muscle activity that is completely out of our hands, supported solely by the gracious provision of God. We cannot survive into the next split second if not for His aid and the strength He supplies.

God is everything we are not. He makes no mistakes. He's not indebted to anyone, doesn't owe us anything. Nothing ever just occurs to God. Nothing ever surprises Him. He never has to scramble to come up with a solution. He has no sudden starts or emergency situations. This One who cares for us so completely doesn't have to follow current events— He determines and foresees all events—past, present, and future. He never needs to stop and figure out what His next move will be.

So . . .

Women of God, why would we ever need to get bent out of shape by something that's not going our way? Why would we doubt that God is not only fully capable of providing our need, but that He has seen this challenge coming from far away and has been preparing us for it all along . . . that He is even now accomplishing "a thousand different things" through this very process of events?

Believing this leaves no place for doubt, or fear, or anger, or second-guessing, or disputing God's choices. He is God, and we are not. It's not up to us to understand it all. And why should we? We are covered and cared for by One who is sovereign and all-wise, whose thoughts are unfathomable, the depths of whose ways are impossible to plumb.

*"How unsearchable . . . how inscrutable . . ."*

And yet, we must acknowledge that His ways do not always *seem* right to human reason or sense. At times they can be hard, painful, or confusing (to us, not to Him!). In fact, we stand in a long line of sisters who have stood before the imponderable ways of God and been faced with the option of either demanding an answer or living in submitted trust.

- Sarah, whose husband's wavering faith put her life in jeopardy on at least two occasions
- Ruth, widowed in a strange land, becoming the object of racism and hardship

- Hannah, suffering years of infertility, taunts, and unfulfilled longings for a child
- Mary, facing an unplanned, teenage pregnancy, having her soul pierced as she offered up her Son for the sins of the world

God's ways for you—just as His ways for these women—will not always make sense to your human reasoning. They may mean physical challenges, weakness, weariness, aging, disease. His plan for your life may include financial hardship, family difficulties, infertility, a special-needs child. It may mean a parent with Alzheimer's, unfulfilled longings for a mate, loss of a husband or child, a prodigal son or daughter. The list could go on and on, taking you down paths you never envisioned, drawing a story line you'd never have scripted.

But we stand in this line with the Lord Jesus, for whom the ways of God meant divesting Himself of His rights, experiencing rejection and ridicule on a scale never known by anyone before or since, then ultimately enduring a cruel death on the cross. *"How inscrutable."*

Your circumstances may be difficult. They may be hard to understand—incomprehensible to your feeble sense. It may seem that His plan is not working; you can't imagine how the outcome could be anything but bleak.

But you can be assured that God doesn't make mistakes. He has an eternal purpose in mind—a plan for the display of His glory throughout all the universe. He is working out that plan, and you are a part of it.

You don't have to know what He's doing. Or why.

The fact is, *He* knows. And that's all that really matters.

And if you trust Him, in time, you will thank Him for the treasures that have resulted from those trials. As a friend going through a deeply trying season with young adult children confided to me recently with tears, "If I hadn't been through this, I wouldn't know God the way I do. I wouldn't desire Him the way I do."

### He's Everything

Paul's towering statements of truth can lead to only one conclusion: *"For from him and through him and to him are all things"* (Romans 11:36). Everything finds its true meaning and purpose in *God's* meaning and purpose.

This is why true womanhood results in a God-centered life and perspective, a God-centered worldview, eternally tethered to who God is and His sovereign, inscrutable ways.

If you're not there or are unwilling to go there—if you're resisting the call of God for true womanhood—your life will be set adrift on a sea of shifting emotions and unruly ways of thinking. You are inviting depression and anger. You are tempting bitterness and confusion. You are fueling a mind-set that will stay in constant disarray, with no reference point to provide any kind of stability for your life.

Where you need to be is here: *"From him and through him and to him are all things."* If you're not *there*, you've missed the whole point of your existence.

#### *"From him . . . are all things."*

He is the Source and origin of our existence. We have no life apart from Him. All things were created by Him. That means that every circumstance that touches your life and mine, including even severe loss and testing, comes into our lives through the filter of His sovereign hand. It means that the real issue behind any conflict you're facing is not your husband, your kids, your singleness, or your health. In fact, to resist or resent the situation and circumstances in which you find yourself is ultimately to resent and resist God Himself. *From Him* are all things.

#### *"Through him . . . are all things."*

Not only is He the Source, but He is also the Sustainer, the one who "upholds the universe by the word of his power" (Hebrews 1:3), the one in whom "all things hold together" (Colossians 1:17). If not for His powerful word sustaining the sun, the moon, the stars, and the planets, the entire universe would all fall apart, including (of course) us. So when you feel like you just can't hold things together any longer, guess what? You can't hold *anything* together—not even for a second. But He can. And He does.

### *"To him are all things."*

He is our supreme purpose. He is our goal. He created all things—including you and me—for Himself and His pleasure. How contrary this is to our natural perspective that says "it's all about me." We live as though all things were from *us*, and through *us*, and to *us*, which leaves us depleted, fearful, angry, bitter, confused, and depressed. But God loves us too much to let us continue hurtling toward hopelessness and dissatisfaction. When we oppose His righteous, unsearchable judgments, He lovingly disciplines us as His children until we're back in line with the way things really are, the way He created all things to operate.

Yes, God is the Source of all things, the sovereign Lord and Director of all things, the Sustainer of all things, and the supreme Goal of all things. That means nothing is beyond His ability to control, to transform, and to use for His glory and your good. In His way and His time, even the sinful choices of human beings—those who have wronged and wounded you, and who perhaps continue to cause you harm even as you attempt to reach out in mercy and forgiveness—even these unholy actions will eventually glorify God and demonstrate the greatness of His wisdom, power, and grace. There is simply no escape for anyone from the cosmic reality that *"from him and through him and to him are all things."*

And what is our response? *"To him be glory forever. Amen"* (Romans 11:36). The appropriate response to the fathomless depths of God's wisdom and ways is to step out of the spotlight and turn the spotlight on Him. It is to say, *Amen!*—wholeheartedly affirming our agreement with the Word of God. We believe that our bottomless, unsearchable, all-encompassing Lord is the sum and whole point of everything there is. Therefore, we submit our entire lives to His holy, eternal purposes. *Amen.* Let it be so!

## A True Woman's Response

So what does all this have to do with being a "true woman"? How does it apply to where we live? My friend, this passage has everything to do with being a true woman of God. This is where true women find a refuge for their hearts. In embracing these truths, we discover what true womanhood is all about.

All that we have seen about God and His ways is designed to bring us comfort as well as courage and conviction in our calling as women. There are many implications and applications we could make, but I want to leave you with three simple ones that apply to every Christian woman. I pray that you will grasp them and seek to orient your life around them.

**1)** *A true woman lives a God-centered life.* We live in a self-centered world, but a true woman of God lives a God-centered life. She lives for His glory and pleasure, not her own . . . because it's not about us. It is all, all, all about Him. A God-centered woman embraces the supreme purpose for which she was created. She lives to reflect the beauty and wonder of His ways and to join every created thing in heaven and earth in glorifying and worshiping Him eternally. This is her reason for living. This is what gets her up in the morning and keeps her going through the day. Every day and every moment of every day, she seeks to live with His purposes in view.

Seeing the magnitude of His greatness and fixing our eyes on Him gives a whole new context and perspective for our problems. You may say, "Nancy, you have no idea how big my challenge is. I'm not just imagining it or blowing it out of proportion." Please hear me: I'm not minimizing what you're going through. Compared to what I'm facing right now, your issues may be huge—but not by comparison with the torrent, the river of God's love, mercy, and grace. Our greatest problems, no matter how enormous and unsolvable they may seem, become puny when measured against the vastness of God.

A true woman is more than a good wife and mother, a loyal friend and daughter. More than anything else, she is enthralled with the Lord Jesus Christ—the Pearl of great price, the supreme Treasure of life. He is the center of her universe and her life revolves around Him.

And therefore, a true woman has hope—real, genuine hope—in the midst of a world filled with pain, loss, and uncertainty. A true woman is a God-centered woman.

**2) *A true woman trusts God.*** We live in a fearful world. We know now that our generation is not immune from the same kind of stock market plunges that make us think of grainy, black-and-white film images from the Great Depression. We read of random shooting sprees that erupt in shopping centers or places of business or church services. We see third-graders hustled into lockdown on reports that a gunman has been spotted nearby. And we experience unexpected and life-altering events a lot closer to home that have our own names written on them.

But the true woman doesn't give in to fear. As Proverbs 31:25 says, she "smiles at the future" (NASB), because she knows He's got the whole world in His hands. She knows of a God whose depths never reach bottom, whose ways are beyond finding out. She knows that the One in charge of "all things" can be trusted to know

> *A true woman has hope— real, genuine hope—in the midst of a world filled with pain, loss, and uncertainty.*

what He's doing. He has a plan we would not have scripted, a plan we may not understand, but it is His plan, and His plan is good, wise, and can never be thwarted.

So a true woman accepts His plan as good, though it may not be the way *she* defines good. She knows it's *God* who defines good, so she leans on Him. She depends on Him even in times of prosperity, joy, and plenty. But she also maintains her trustful gratitude in times of pain and hardship, of lack and want, of loneliness, uncertainty, and confusion. She is married to Christ—for better, for worse, for richer, for poorer—not like a paid lover, wanting Him only for what He can give her.

I know life is hard to understand. From our limited frame of reference, it sometimes seems that God doesn't know what He's doing. And though many of us would never dare to speak such words aloud or even consciously think them, many of us are practicing atheists at times, living as if there's no God, or at least wondering if He has really messed things up this time.

A true woman, however, trusts God completely, patiently believing that He is faithful, and that in His way and in His time, His promises will be fulfilled.

Perhaps you're thinking, *It's not God who's messed up—it's me. I'm the one who has failed. I can't see how God's plan for my life could ever be fulfilled.* A true woman trusts that her past failures are not beyond the reach of God's redeeming grace. Unredeemable losses and impossibilities do not exist in the inscrutable mind of God. As Martin Luther succinctly captured it, "God can draw a straight line with a crooked stick," even if those "crooked sticks" are your personal failings, even if they're the sins of a parent, a husband, a child, an employer. Nothing is beyond His plan and repair.

> *The true woman who trusts God doesn't have to strive.*

The way God goes about redeeming this broken world is so very different than the way we would do it. So when we can't understand what He's doing or why He's doing it, it's not our place to challenge or dispute, but rather to humbly bow before His sovereignty, His goodness, His mercy, and His greatness— *"the riches and wisdom and knowledge of God"*—and to align ourselves with His purposes, embracing His will.

The true woman who trusts God doesn't have to strive. She doesn't have to be afraid. She can relinquish control. She doesn't have to manipulate and control the whole wide world (as if we could). She doesn't resent, or resist, or run from the cross. She embraces the cross with faith.

I love the way the eighteenth-century English poet William Cowper expressed the kind of confident trust we see in Romans 11:

God moves in a mysterious way,
His wonders to perform;
He plants his footsteps in the sea,
And rides upon the storm.

Deep in unfathomable mines
Of never failing skill,
He treasures up his bright designs,
And works his sovereign will.

Ye fearful saints, fresh courage take,
The clouds ye so much dread
Are big with mercy, and shall break
In blessings on your head.

Judge not the Lord by feeble sense,
But trust him for his grace;
Behind a frowning providence,
He hides a smiling face.

His purposes will ripen fast,
Unfolding ev'ry hour;
The bud may have a bitter taste,
But sweet will be the flow'r.

Blind unbelief is sure to err,
And scan his work in vain;
God is his own interpreter,
And he will make it plain.

**3)** *A true woman says, "Yes, Lord."* That's basically what Paul goes on to say in the verse that immediately follows our text: "I appeal to you therefore, brothers, by the mercies of God, to present your bodies as a living sacrifice, living and holy and acceptable to God" (Romans 12:1).

A true woman recognizes that her life is not her own. She lives instead for the glory of God. His Word, not her world, becomes her compass. She affirms that His purposes are good and wise, and therefore she follows His leading with the "yes" of full obedience and submission.

The true woman accepts the way God made her, embracing her

God-given design and roles in life, being grateful that He has made her a woman, thankful for the privilege of serving and giving and fulfilling His holy purposes.

She lives intentionally, not just drifting from one meaningless activity to the next, letting the circumstances of life pull her along. She's willing to be like a salmon, swimming upstream, living a counter-cultural life in an unholy world for the glory of God. She's willing to make personal sacrifices, not constantly asking, "What will make me happy?" Rather, she wants to know: "What will please *You,* Lord?" "What will further Your kingdom?" "What will display Your glory?" Her heart attitude is, "If it pleases You, it pleases me." The true woman reflects the spirit of Mary of Nazareth when she said in response to God's calling, "I am the servant of the Lord; let it be to me according to your word" (Luke 1:38).

*"Yes, Lord."*

To say, "Yes, Lord," means saying no to a lot of other things:

- "no" to bitterness
- "no" to self-centeredness
- "no" to whining
- "no" to complaining
- "no" to pining
- "no" to resisting, resenting, running from the will of God

But it means saying yes to a lot more:

- "yes" to forgiving those who have sinned against us
- "yes" to receiving God's forgiveness for ourselves
- "yes" to repentance
- "yes" to serving
- "yes" to embracing God's choices for our lives
- "yes" to trusting Him with our circumstances
- "yes" to finding and fulfilling His purposes

Living a God-centered life, trusting Him even when we don't understand, responding to Him with a heart that always says "Yes, Lord"—this is no easy way to travel. The road that winds through this kind of lifestyle can be steep and scary at times. But we walk by faith, not by sight.

And if you will keep pressing on by His grace, I assure you the day will come when you will get to the summit, as Paul did in Romans 11. Then, you'll look back at the trails you have scaled by His grace; you'll look around at the scenery, amazed at the unsearchable depths of God.

The sight will be glorious and you will say, "Ah, I see! It all makes sense now. . . . Why was I so anxious? Why did I fret? Why did I become bitter and angry? Why did I despise my husband for making my life so difficult? I see now that he was an instrument in the hand of God to fulfill God's holy, eternal purposes. . . ."

We will look back on the path we have climbed, with vision and clarity we cannot possibly have now. And our hearts will cry out, "Oh Lord my God, You have done all things well. . . . How great Thou art!"

For sure, there will be those long nights and days when the summit seems hopelessly far away, when all you can see is trouble and danger, when you're not sure why He's put you in such a tight place.

For all those days, I offer you Romans 11:33–36—the depths, the riches, the wisdom, the knowledge of God. His unsearchable judgments. His inscrutable ways. You can fall back into His sovereignty, sure of His love, and proclaim with Paul, even through your tears and troubles, *"To him be glory forever. Amen."*

# PART TWO

# the battle for
# true womanhood

*The greatest influence on earth whether for good or for evil,
is possessed by woman.
Let us study the history of by-gone ages, the state of
barbarism and civilisation;
of the east and the west; of Paganism and Christianity;
of antiquity and the middle ages; of the mediaeval and modern times;
and we shall find that there is nothing which more decidedly
separates them than the condition of woman.*[1]

— ADOLPHE MONOD (1802–1856)

# you've come a long way, **baby!**

## MARY A. KASSIAN

In the late 1960s, the Philip Morris Tobacco Company introduced Virginia Slims as a "women's only" cigarette, launching it with the now well-known slogan, *"You've come a long way, baby!"* The print ads were marked by staged, old-fashioned, black-and-white photos picturing the miserable state of women in the 1900s, prior to the first women's movement, juxtaposed against full-color photos of far happier, modern women demonstrating their emancipation from male dominance . . . by smoking Virginia Slims.

In one such ad, three small black-and-white scenes depict an arrogant, overweight husband impatiently ringing a bell, demanding that his servile wife respond to his every need. The caption reads, "With this ring, I thee wed. Ring for supper. Ring for paper. Ring for slippers." The happy, modern, Virginia Slims woman pictured in the forefront rejects the traditional "male-defined" institution of marriage. Man will not be the head of *her* home. *"You've come a long way, baby!"*

The caption of another ad announces, "Back then, education taught men to run the world and women to run the house." It shows bored women sitting at old-fashioned desks learning about home economics. The blackboard proclaims that there will be a laundry quiz on Tuesday, and that their homework consists of several cooking and cleaning assignments. The Virginia Slims woman on the adjoining page stands in marked contrast to this outdated concept of female domesticity. She is enlightened. She knows that running a house and looking after children is a low-class, unfulfilling, demeaning job, unsuitable for someone with a university education. She's determined to get out of the house and do something really important—like run the world! *"You've come a long way, baby!"*

The old-fashioned, black-and-white scene of a third ad depicts several women working hard at typewriters and desks behind their male boss, who thumbs his lapels and takes all the credit for their efforts. The caption reads: "Virginia Slims looks back upon the self-made man (and all the women who made him possible)." The smug Virginia Slims woman in the foreground holds the lapels of *her* business suit in the same manner as the boastful male boss. But there's no one in the background propping her up. She's a self-made woman. She makes *herself* possible! *"You've come a long way, baby!"*

A final ad features a large, colorless photo of two policemen forcibly removing a woman from a public beach for wearing an immodest bathing suit. The woman is screaming, "You just wait! Someday we'll be able to wear any bathing suit we want. Someday we'll be able to vote. Someday we'll even have our own cigarette!" The policeman retorts, "That'll be the day." But the happy, enlightened Virginia Slims woman in the forefront has the last word. She doesn't doubt there *will* be a day when she has the right to set her own standards of sexual conduct, morality, and propriety—a day when she dismantles and rewrites all the rules. *"You've come a long way, baby!"*

## We've Come a Long Way

Women truly have come a long way in the past fifty years. But a long way isn't necessarily a good way or the right way.

Up until the middle of the last century, Western culture as a whole generally embraced a Judeo-Christian perspective on gender and sexuality as well as the purpose and structure of the family. Heterosexual marriage, marital fidelity, and the bearing and nurturing of children in an intact family unit were highly valued concepts—the norm of societal practice. Most agreed that the primary responsibility of the male was to lead, protect, and provide for his family, while the primary responsibility of the female was to nurture and care for her children and home. Differences between male and female were accepted and seldom questioned.

Furthermore, for both men and women, their sense of duty and responsibility to family was greater than the pursuit of personal fulfillment. Though they may not have been able to identify the source of their values, most individuals had a sense of what it meant to be a man or a woman. They understood the appropriate outworking of gender roles and relationships.

Not anymore. We've "come a long way, baby." And the speed and magnitude of force with which this understanding has been deconstructed is astonishing.

Consider the cultural image of women in the 1950s represented by the popular TV sitcom *Leave It to Beaver*. The Cleaver family exemplified the idealized suburban family. In this television series, four ideals were presented as requisites for a happy life, both for women and men: education (Ward and June Cleaver both had college degrees), marriage, children, and hard work. In typical late-fifties fashion, June worked hard at home all day taking care of her household and serving in the community while her husband, Ward, worked hard outside of the home to financially support the family. June was there with fresh-baked cookies and a tall, cold glass of milk when her children, Wally and Beaver, arrived home from school. When Ward walked in the door after work, June, wearing a pretty dress, greeted him with a smile and a kiss, a clean house, and a hot meal on the table for supper.

June and Ward Cleaver were both happy and content. In fact, adults in the *Leave It to Beaver* sitcom who didn't or couldn't attain the cultural ideals of education, marriage, children, and hard work were the ones depicted as being troubled or missing out. Mrs. Mondello, for example—the mom of Beaver's friend Larry—had a husband who was frequently out of town on business. She was presented as an unhappy, exasperated parent struggling singlehandedly to raise a son, sometimes depending on Ward to help discipline him. Spinsters like prim, rich Aunt Martha were presented as irksome and interfering, while Uncle Billy, the globe-trotting, yarn-spinning bachelor; free-loading Jeff, the tramp; and Andy, the alcoholic handyman, were depicted from the happily married viewpoint of the series as having missed the mark in life. In the one episode dealing with divorce, the event is depicted as a horrible tragedy, having solely negative effects on children and adults alike.

As the *Leave It to Beaver* sitcom suggests, life for women truly was vastly different fifty years ago than it is today. Consider these real-life observations from the 1950s:

- Getting married was the norm. Almost *everyone* got married. The average age was twenty for gals and twenty-two for guys.
- Once married, it was expected that the couple would have children, and that the husband would financially support his wife so she could stay at home and care for them during their childhood years.
- The divorce rate was low. People were expected to remain married and to make their marriages work. Divorce was considered a terrible tragedy.
- If a divorce did occur, and if there were children involved, the courts expected the ex-husband to financially support the wife in a homemaking role, because society considered it vitally important that children have a mom at home.
- Chastity, virginity, and fidelity were virtues; sex outside of a marriage relationship was shameful.
- Scarcely anyone lived common-law, for it carried the stigma of "living in sin." Furthermore, it was unthinkable and totally improper for a single woman to have a male roommate. The number

of couples living together common-law before marriage was so small that statistics for this phenomenon were not even recorded.

- Having a child outside of wedlock was also considered shameful. (Today, one American child is born outside of marriage every twenty-five seconds. More than 40 percent of children will go to sleep tonight in homes in which their fathers do not live.)
- Only 30 percent of all women were employed outside of the home in 1960, and many of those worked part-time. Only rarely was a woman professionally employed if her children were younger than school age.
- Children were highly desired, highly valued, and highly welcomed additions to both family and community.
- There was no birth control pill.
- Abortion was illegal.
- Pornography, rape, homosexuality, sexual perversion, sexual addiction, and sexually transmitted diseases were uncommon and rarely encountered.
- Men saw it as their responsibility to protect and provide for the women and children under their care.
- Women saw it as their responsibility to support their husbands and focus on raising children in a stable, nurturing, loving environment. Their professional careers took secondary status to their primary and more important career of raising and nurturing the next generation.
- Though certainly not attained by all, the idyllic, *Leave It to Beaver* pattern of morality, marriage, family, and home was upheld by society as the ideal.

That was the world into which I was born, some fifty years ago. So I can say from firsthand experience—as perhaps you can too—and with absolute, undeniable accuracy, *"We've come a long way, baby."*

So have our ideas about womanhood.

By the late 1960s, the image of June Cleaver being happy at home in her role as a wife and mother had fallen by the wayside, replaced by the 1970s Mary Tyler Moore image of a perky single woman in her thirties, pursuing a career at a television station. *The Mary Tyler Moore Show* was lauded as a television breakthrough because it portrayed the first independent, attractive career woman as the central character. Yet the focus of the show was on her career, not on her association with men. She was truly on her own, with no recurring father, boyfriend, fiancé, or husband looking out for her. With each episode, the show's theme song proudly alluded to her autonomy, her independence, and her ability to survive just fine without a man: "You're going to make it after all!"

In the 1980s, television introduced us to Murphy Brown, an investigative journalist and news anchor for *FYI*, a fictional TV newsmagazine. In contrast to the gentle sweetness of Mary Tyler Moore's character, Murphy Brown was loud-mouthed, brash, driven, self-assured, self-absorbed, and highly opinionated. She was a divorcée and a proud atheist. During the course of the series, Murphy became pregnant but chose not to marry her baby's father. Naturally a man would cramp her style. Instead, she left the baby in the care of a revolving door of nannies so she could pursue her career. The child was merely a side plot in a story line that revolved around Murphy's self-actualization in the workplace.

In the midnineties, enter Ellen—a woman who owned her own independent bookstore. Ellen lived with a man, but their relationship was merely platonic. She wasn't sexually attracted to him; he was just her roommate. Gradually, however, we discovered that Ellen wasn't attracted to men at all. She was a lesbian—a woman-identified woman with the right to define her own sexuality and her own morality. And no one had the right to judge her for it! As the cover of *TV Guide* lauded, Ellen was "OUT—and in charge!"—as are virtually all the women portrayed in the media in the past decade. From children's cartoons to television series to movies, women in popular media are now portrayed as having an "in charge, don't-need-a-guy, I'm-powerful, traditional-marriage-and-family-and-morals-are-outdated, I-have-the-right-to-rule, how-dare-you-tell-me-what-to-do" mentality.

We've now been thoroughly indoctrinated with the message that when it comes to relationships, women can make their own rules. They can sleep around, hook up, be in casual or long-term relationships, live common-law, get married or remain single, get divorced, get pregnant, have a baby (being married is inconsequential) or abort it, have men as roommates, have sex with men and/or women, and participate in virtually any type of behavior they choose. The sitcom *Friends* was based on the premise that all of these are equally valid choices. A woman can set her own standards and dictate the terms of her relationship with men. And as long as she's "nice" about it, and true to herself, it really doesn't matter what she does. Who are *we* to judge?

The epitome of this mind-set is reflected in a recent popular sitcom for and about women: *Sex and the City*. Selfhood and sisterhood are what it's all about. As long as women are loyal to themselves and to their female buddies, they're on the right track. They can be single or married, lesbian, heterosexual, or any combination thereof. They can be promiscuous, perverted, immoral, have sex as a onesome, twosome, threesome, or room-some. They can be loud, arrogant, vulgar, crude, and crass, but if they stand up for themselves and for other women, and if they're caring and nice underneath, then they're okay. In the new worldview, men are whiny, needy, not too bright, and totally unreliable. They are marginalized and emasculated—used, regarded, and discarded like Kleenex from a box. (The *Sex and the City* character Charlotte only hesitates a moment before giving up her engagement ring to help her girlfriend pay for the down payment on a house.)

Nowadays, the height of empowered womanhood is to live a self-serving, self-righteous, neurotic, narcissistic, superficial, and adulterous life. The main character in *Sex and the City* wraps it up well when she counsels

> *We've now been thoroughly indoctrinated with the message that when it comes to relationships, women can make their own rules.*

55

women that "the most exciting, challenging, and significant relationship of all is the one you have with yourself."

So in a few short decades—in the span of my lifetime—the ideal of a happy, fulfilled woman has gone from one who values and serves her children, her husband, and her community, to one who serves and exalts herself, sees men as dispensable, and considers children to be optional add-ons to her quest for fulfillment.

Which begs the question: How did this happen?

The factors are many and complex, but a large piece of the puzzle can be attributed to the philosophy of feminism.

## The Feminist Revolution

Feminism is a distinct philosophy that shook the underpinnings of society in the early 1960s like a tsunamic earthquake shaking the ocean's floor. Feminism is indeed an "ism"—like atheism, humanism, Marxism, existentialism, or postmodernism. The "ism" indicates that we're talking about a particular philosophical theory, a doctrine, a system of principles and ideas.

It's important to understand that feminism encompasses much more than the cultural phenomenon of the women's rights movement. It's more than just "yesterday's fashion"—a neglected piece of our past hanging like the hippy beads in the back of our mother's closets. It's more than women having the right to an abortion, the right to vote, or the choice to pursue a career. Feminism is a distinct worldview with its own ideologies, values, and ways of thinking. And whether or not you know it or care to admit it, feminism is a philosophy that has profoundly affected virtually every woman, man, and child alive in the Western world today.

Some may think that an intellectual foray into past philosophy, like the one we're taking together in this chapter, is an exercise in futility. But it's the student of history who both understands current culture and is equipped to envision a path for the future. We need to know where we've come from and how we got to this point if we hope to determine where we go from here.

This is a biblical way of approaching history. During a time of national turmoil, the people of ancient Israel were served by the men of Issachar, men who, according to 1 Chronicles 12:32, "had understanding of the times, to know what Israel ought to do." My purpose in this overview is to help you "understand the times" so that God can raise us up as a holy Issachar generation of women in our day. Women who hold the knowledge of our times in one hand, and who hold the truth, clarity, and charity of the Word of God in the other. Women whose hearts are broken over the gender confusion and the spiritual, emotional, relational carnage of our day. Women who (like those men of old) "know" what we, the church, "ought to do."

So I'm going to take you back to the 1950s—back to the days of *Leave It to Beaver*—and paint some broad brushstrokes to show you how the philosophy of feminism developed and was integrated into culture.

First, a bit of historical background. Geopolitically, the world of the 1950s was witnessing an era of revolution. The American, French, and Russian Revolutions of earlier eras had each been based on the enlightenment idea that all people are equal, that no one group has an inherent right to dominate and rule another group. The word "revolution" itself (from the Latin *revolutio*) means "a turnaround," entailing a fundamental change in power that takes place in a relatively short period of time. In the late 1940s and 1950s, the world witnessed revolutions in India, Korea, China, Hungary, Iraq, and Cuba. In all these revolutions, the ruling class was overthrown through violence or civil disobedience by the class they had ruled and sometimes oppressed.

This revolutionary fervor and the fight for individual rights steadily spread from political to social structures. Workers demanded their rights and formed unions—then went on strike if their demands weren't met. College students marched against oppressive educational establishments. Attention was drawn to the racial inequity between blacks and whites when in 1955, Rosa Parks refused to give up her seat on the bus, and the Civil Rights movement was born.

But that wasn't all. During the 1950s, a female French philosopher, Simone de Beauvoir, proposed that modern society was also in need of a revolution in gender roles.

De Beauvoir argued that in the relationship between male and female, men were the ruling class, and women were the lower "second sex." She believed that in order for women to live as full human beings, they needed to demand their rights, collectively rebel against men, and overthrow all the societal structures that men had constructed to keep women in a state of servitude. Specifically, de Beauvoir proposed that in order to gain equality with men, women needed to get out of the home and intentionally deconstruct Judeo-Christian ideas about marriage, motherhood, and morality.

In the late 1950s, American political activist and journalist Betty Friedan picked up on de Beauvoir's thinking. She constructed a questionnaire for the fifteen-year reunion of her graduating class, asking her college-educated female colleagues about the level of happiness and fulfillment they experienced in their marriages and their roles as wives and mothers. Friedan detected undercurrents of discontent and dissatisfaction in their answers.

In the following months she interviewed dozens of other women. And from all of these combined responses, Friedan concluded that a discrepancy did indeed exist between what society told women would make them happy and fulfilled, and how happy and fulfilled they actually felt. In her resulting book, published in 1963, Friedan argued that women were trying to conform to a religious, male-dictated image of womanhood—the *Leave It to Beaver* ideal she called the "feminine mystique"—but that doing so left them with vague feelings of emptiness, yearning, and wanting something more.

Friedan proposed that a gnawing sense of unhappiness with woman's role was a common female problem, albeit one with no name, concluding that the role itself was to blame for woman's discontent. So like de Beauvoir, Friedan suggested that in order to find fulfillment, American women should begin to question, challenge, and rebel against the accepted role of wife and mother and traditional thoughts about morality. According to Friedan, a woman could only be fulfilled if she had a life plan that included education, a career, and work that was of "serious importance to society."[1] (Homemaking and raising children were not thought to be of "serious importance.") To be equal to men, each woman needed to move beyond the restrictive shackles of the male-defined, male-serving, traditional role of wife and mother, and *name herself* by developing a vision for her own future. She needed to reject the image of womanhood that had purportedly been constructed and perpetuated by men. Woman needed to claim the authority to define her own existence.

> *According to feminism, the only hope for woman's happiness and self-fulfillment lay in rejecting a male-defined, Judeo-Christian worldview.*

Friedan summarized the underlying precept of feminism when she declared, "We [women] need and can trust no other authority than our own personal truth!"[2] According to feminism, the only hope for woman's happiness and self-fulfillment lay in rejecting a male-defined, Judeo-Christian worldview and convincing herself to define her own truth.

Alvin Toffler, author of *Future Shock*, called Friedan's *The Feminine Mystique* "the book that pulled the trigger on history."[3] And indeed, once woman accepted this basic premise of needing and trusting no other authority than her own, she set her foot on a path that would rapidly take her—and ultimately the whole of society—in a direction diametrically opposed to the heart and purposes and ways of God.

Throughout the 1960s, de Beauvoir's and Friedan's writings began to gain popularity among North American women. Many were evidently experiencing inner feelings of frustration and discontentment, eagerly yearning for the "something more" proffered by these feminist pioneers. A problem had been exposed. Feminists were convinced that it was *the* problem. And although they had not yet found a word to adequately describe it, they felt confident that therein resided the cause of woman's malaise.

In the late 1960s, feminist author Kate Millett used the term "patriarchy" to describe the "problem without a name."[4] Patriarchy derives its origin from two Greek words: *pater*, meaning "father," and *arche*, meaning "rule." Patriarchy was to be understood as the "rule of the father," and was used to describe both the dominance of the male as well as the inferiority and subservience of the female.

Feminists argued that patriarchy wasn't just an abstract concept of men having more power and authority than women. It was a pattern woven throughout every aspect of culture and thought. Patriarchy had dictated the whole of Western culture's family, social, political, and religious structures. Patriarchy was at the root of its social etiquette, customs, rituals, traditions, and laws. Patriarchy was woven throughout its entire system of education and the economic division of labor. All of these things were responsible for keeping men in a dominant position (and therefore women in a subservient position) throughout human history.

This conclusion could mean only one thing: in order to attain woman's equality, every aspect of belief and culture would need to be changed. Only the demise and redefinition of all patriarchal structures would lead to her freedom. Only in breaking free from traditional Judeo-Christian roles and rules would woman find meaning and self-fulfillment.

And thus, the trigger was pulled.

## Renaming Self

In the first phase of feminism, women claimed the right to name themselves, to redefine their own existence. Their goal was to become more like men and to shed the differences that made them weak and vulnerable to exploitation. Women began to dress like men; to smoke, drink, and swear like men; to claim sexual freedom and participation in the work force on the same basis as men; and to control the biological functions that made them different from men.

Newly established feminist groups, such as NOW (the National Organization for Women), began lobbying and demonstrating publicly in order to further the feminist agenda, which consisted of five main tenets: 1) full self-determination, 2) freedom from biological distinctions, 3) economic independence, 4) total and equal integration into the workforce, and 5) sexual freedom.

To that end they fought for an Equal Rights Amendment, liberalized divorce laws, legalization of abortion, reproductive technology, Planned Parenthood, state-funded day care, pay equity, affirmative action, women in the military, and lesbian rights. They picketed outside *The New York Times* building in opposition to the male/female segregated help-wanted ads run by the paper. They organized demonstrations against the firing of stewardesses. They demonstrated on Madison Avenue against TV soap operas. They organized a splashy protest of the Miss America contest that played across nearly every television screen in the country. They boycotted, picketed, lobbied, demonstrated, sued, marched, and engaged in all kinds of nonviolent civil disobedience.

But although awareness of the women's movement was growing, allegiance to the feminist perspective was still not widespread. Feminist theorists concluded that women as a whole needed enlightenment. They needed to discover how oppressed they really were.

Then along came a tool—discovered quite inadvertently—that effectively convinced women of the rightness of the feminist cause. This proved to be the key to igniting their revolution.

Feminists in New York discovered that if they gathered women together in small groups, and got those women talking about their personal hurts and grievances against men, then *all* the women in the group would begin to get upset and bitter against men—even those who initially had no identifiable issues. With direction, the group's anger could then be channeled into personal and political activism. Collectively, the whole group could be empowered to rebel against men, thereby becoming actively committed to the feminist cause.

Kathie Sarachild, a feminist activist in New York, learned that this new technique was called "consciousness raising," and that it wasn't actually "new" at all. Consciousness raising was a political technique that had been used by the revolutionary army of Mao Tse-tung, whose slogan was, "*Speak* bitterness to *recall* bitterness. *Speak* pain to *recall* pain." To promote discord and instability in a village, Mao's political revolutionaries would gather townswomen together to discuss the crimes their men had committed against them, encouraging the women to "speak bitterness and pain." Initial reluctance gave way to collective anger as woman after woman recounted stories of rape by their landlords, of being sold as concubines, of physical abuse by their husbands and fathers-in-law.

> *As the women vented their bitterness, they experienced a newfound strength and resolve that empowered them to corporate action.*

As the women vented their bitterness, they experienced a newfound strength and resolve that empowered them to corporate action. In one village, for example, a peasant man was physically pummeled by an entire group of women because his wife had complained to the others about the way she had been treated. The revolutionaries had incited the women to speak bitterness. As a result, the women grew angry and rebellious. They went home and demanded personal and political change. That's how Mao Tse-tung fueled his revolution.

In the fall of 1968, Sarachild organized "A Guide and Manifesto to Consciousness Raising" (CR) and presented it to the first national Women's Liberation Conference, held in Chicago. She proposed that the feminist movement use this political technique to activate a broad scale gender revolution, arguing that through consciousness-raising groups, small sparks of personal unhappiness could be fanned into an inferno of corporate discontent and political action. The small group dynamic was the most radical, effective tool for leading a woman to a personal "aha!" moment—the moment when she sees that all the problems in the world are due to the rule of men, and that traditional rules and roles need to be discarded in order for women to achieve equality and personal fulfillment.

Consciousness raising encouraged women to change their beliefs and behavior patterns, to make new demands in interpersonal relationships, to insist on their own rights, and to support the women's movement, thereby consummating their new awareness with political action. These groups spread like wildfire. Soon there were "CR-Rap" groups in homes, in community centers, in churches, in YWCAs, and in many places of business.

Perhaps you remember an old Fabergé shampoo commercial that started with a picture of just one woman. Then as her image steadily multiplied, she chirped, "I told two friends about Fabergé Organic Shampoo . . . and *they* told two friends, and *they* told two friends . . . and so on . . . and so on . . ." Soon the screen was filled with hundreds upon hundreds of copies of her image. That's the power of word-of-mouth.

And that's exactly how feminism spread.

Only about two hundred women attended the first national women's conference in Chicago in 1968. But with the help of consciousness raising, incessant media coverage, and generous government funding, women all across the continent caught the revolutionary fervor and began to claim the right to name and define themselves. By 1970, twenty *thousand* women marched proudly down New York's Fifth Avenue, identifying themselves as part of the women's liberation movement. Friedan summed up the tenor of the occasion when, at the conclusion of the march, she blazed:

> In the religion of my ancestors, there was a prayer that Jewish men said every morning. They prayed, "Thank thee, Lord, that I was not born a woman." Today . . . all women are going to be able to say . . . "Thank thee, Lord, that I *was* born a woman, for this day. . . ." After tonight, the politics of this nation will never be the same again. . . . There is no way any man, woman, or child can escape the nature of our revolution.[5]

## Renaming the World

Women as a group were having their eyes opened—their consciousness raised—to the commonality of their experience. They were now a sisterhood. The effect was an internal, personal legitimization of the differences found in women. Whereas the first phase of the movement viewed women's differences as weaknesses, the second phase viewed women's differences as a source of pride and confidence. Feminists began to believe that not only were women "just as good as" men. They were in fact "better" than men—a shift in mind-set epitomized by Helen Reddy's 1972 Grammy-winning song "I Am Woman," which topped the pop charts of that time. Looking back, I can still hear the roar, "in numbers too big to ignore . . . I am strong, I am invincible, I am woman!"

Feminists reasoned that women not only had the right to name *themselves* but also had the right to name the *world*. In the words of Reddy's song, they had to "make their brothers understand." Men had gotten everything so very wrong. History was but a legacy of arbitrary, male-defined meaning: *his*-story. And it was time for that to change. From economics to politics, psychology to linguistics, relationships to religion, women needed to challenge and change that which men had both constructed and construed for their own benefit. Women needed to look at the world through the lens of female experience and come up with new values and definitions. What's more, they needed to reeducate all people to think according to the new feminist paradigm. The formation of feminist-driven government agencies, combined with federal funding and media momentum, ensured that they were able to do just that.

Thus, their leaders embarked on an intensive strategy of feminist research and education they called "Woman-Centered Analysis" and "Women's Studies." This was essentially the study of the world based on women's own perceptions and experiences. The National Women's Studies Association (NWSA), which coordinated and spearheaded the effort, noted that their aim was to promote "a breakthrough in consciousness and knowledge which will transform individuals, institutions, relationships, and, ultimately, the whole of society."[6] It was not long, naturally, before college courses sprang up across the country exploring the rights of women, their status in society, the discrimination they experienced in public roles and private lives, as well as the male gender bias prevalent in culture, literature, and learning.

The explosion of woman-centered analysis and women's studies in the 1970s was absolutely staggering. Prior to 1969, there were *no* women's studies courses on college campuses. Ten years later, the number of women's studies courses had mushroomed to well over thirty thousand. Women's studies had been established as a distinct discipline with degrees available at bachelor, master, and doctoral levels. Feminist journals, publications, and magazines (such as *Ms.*) flooded the popular market.

Efforts by the NWSA led to the introduction of feminist theories into all areas and all levels of education. Educators modified kindergarten books, grade-school curricula, continuing education courses, and technical school syllabi to reflect a feminist worldview. The values and beliefs of feminism began to be presented in newspapers, periodicals, newscasts, and television programming. By the end of the 1970s, it was difficult to find any medium of communication uninfluenced by feminist thought.

Feminists often refer to the 1970s as the Golden Age of feminism. At the opening of the decade, their theory was espoused by a small handful of radicals. By the close, however, it had been disseminated to the point where to some extent, it had influenced every member of society. As the eighties dawned, many women had claimed the feminist right to name themselves and their world. And a few, both in secular and religious circles, had started to claim another right: the right to name *God*.

## Renaming God

When Helen Reddy accepted the Grammy award for her "I Am Woman" song, she proudly proclaimed, "I'd like to thank God because *She* made everything possible." Betty Friedan, earlier that year, had predicted that the great debate of the next decade would be "Is God He?" Feminists had proven successful at naming themselves and their world, and in the final phase of feminist thought development, they turned their attention to naming God. The progression was logical. For if woman has the right to define her own existence, as well as the right to define what men and the world ought to look like, then she surely has the right to redefine God too.

> *If the male God of the Bible is unacceptable to women, then who or what is god?*

Feminists argued that the "male" God of the Bible was bad for women. For "if God is male, then the male is god." They argued that religion and the God of the Bible were the primary tools men had used throughout history to keep themselves in a position of power, and women in a position of servitude.

But if the God of the Bible is unacceptable to women, then who or what is god? According to feminism, women get to decide—which ultimately means that they themselves are god. The feminist metaphysic teaches that each woman contains divinity within her own being. New Age philosophy, Wicca, and goddess worship are all expressions of the feminist spirituality that arose in the 1980s and 1990s. According to feminism, each woman is her own goddess, part of the elemental, female creative power of the universe.

Have you ever wondered why advertisers nowadays would name a new women's shaver after a goddess, marketing their product as being able to provide stubble-free legs worthy of the goddess in you? This idea didn't come out of a vacuum. It reflects the fundamental idea of feminism that women have the inherent right to name themselves, the world, and God.

## God's Right to Name

Again, the underlying premise of feminism is that "women need and can trust no other authority than our own personal truth." Feminism teaches that women ought not to bow down and submit to any external power.

But that's not the message of the Bible. God created us. And He created us male and female. This fact is not inconsequential. It *means* something. The Bible informs us that there was an essential difference in the manner and purpose behind the creation of the two sexes. The New Testament reiterates that there are basic differences between men and women that are to be honored as part of God's design. By refusing to honor these differences, or by defiantly stating that it cannot be so, we are claiming the right to define our own existence. But according to the Bible, that is a right which belongs to God alone. It is God who made the earth and created mankind upon it, and we do not have the right to question the wisdom of His directives for our lives. God spoke through Isaiah:

> *Woe to him who quarrels with his Maker, to him who is but a potsherd* [a broken piece of pottery] *among the potsherds on the ground. Does the clay say to the potter, "What are you making?" Does your work say, "He has no hands"? . . . Concerning things to come, do you question me about my children, or give me orders about the work of my hands? It is I who made the earth and created mankind upon it.* (Isaiah 45:9, 11b–12a NIV)

The apostle Paul repeats the admonition in Romans:

> *But who are you, O man, to talk back to God? "Shall what is formed say to him who formed it, 'Why did you make me like this?'" Does not the potter have the right to make out of the same lump of clay some pottery for noble purposes and some for common use?* (Romans 9:20–21 NIV)

The Creator fashioned the two sexes differently. This is a fact we dare not overlook nor trivialize. In 1 Corinthians 11 we are told that "man did not come from woman, but woman from man; neither was man created for woman, but woman for man" (vv. 8–9 NIV). Furthermore, "woman is not independent of man, nor is man independent of woman. For as woman came from man, so also man is born of woman. But everything comes from God" (vv. 11–12 NIV). Numerous other texts in the Bible deal with differences in both the creation and functions of male and female.

The two sexes were simply created differently. And the Bible provides important information as to how these differences are to be evidenced. It does not, as some have argued, provide a stereotyped checklist of *which* sex does *what* (like, men fix the cars, women do the baking), but it does provide broad foundational principles for the proper functioning of male-female relationships. The biblical framework helps us to know and understand ourselves as men and women.

Our identity as male and female also has an important symbolic aspect. It teaches us about the relationship between ourselves as God's people (the church) and God. It also teaches us something of the relationships within the Godhead itself. The reality of who we are, how the world works, and who God is, is not hidden. It is revealed to us through the symbols and images of God, as well as through His creation of male and female. If we lose these fundamental images, we lose ourselves.

Feminists recognize that the act of *naming* conveys power to those who do it. When women claim the right to name themselves, they remove themselves from God's authority, claiming what is rightfully His as their own. This is the crux, as well as the foundational danger of feminist philosophy. As Christians, we must allow God to name Himself, to name His world, and to name male and female. This belief contains the only hope for getting life right. The only hope for discovering our true identity and purpose. The only hope for untangling the gnarled, knotted mess that sin has made of gender and relationships. The only hope for experiencing ever greater measures of healing and joy. And above all, the only hope for reflecting and exalting the beauty of the gospel and the glory of God.

## Saying "Yes!" to True Womanhood

So what's the answer to the question feminism posed almost fifty years ago? It was a spiritual question: "What is going to bring women happiness and fulfillment and joy in life?" Do we turn back the clock and return to the 1950s? Is it true that a woman will only find satisfaction when she finds the perfect man—when she's a mom and housewife, when she's safely situated in a station wagon and a home surrounded by a white picket fence? Or do we rely on the feminist formula for fulfillment—woman's unmitigated freedom to pursue fulfillment in career and sex, controlling and discarding men and doing what we please?

History has shown that the *Leave It to Beaver* ideal is not the one that will satisfy. There is no man on the face of this earth who can completely fulfill the desires of a woman's heart. Being a wife and a mom is a great calling and privilege, but it doesn't satisfy our deepest needs.

> *History has shown that the* **Leave It to Beaver** *ideal is not the one that will satisfy.*

The feminist solution, however, won't satisfy either. The longings of our hearts will not be met when we look to careers and sex and self-determination for fulfillment. We won't find any more happiness striving for the modern-day ideal than our 1950s sisters did by striving for the ideal of their time. No, in order to find fulfillment as a woman, you and I need to turn our hearts toward the right target. We need to turn to the One for whom we were created and to whom all our yearnings point—the Lord Jesus Christ—and say "yes!" to Him.

We tend to reduce the discussion about womanhood to peripheral questions: her marital status, whether she has children, her education and career choices, whether she works outside of the home, her use of birth control, whether she educates her children at home or sends them off to school, the type of clothes or make-up she wears. These questions are not unimportant, but they are not the essence of true womanhood.

The heart of true womanhood is to understand and agree with the purposes of our Creator. A woman is a true woman when her heart says yes to God.

Feminism promised women happiness and fulfillment. But it hasn't delivered. The new generation is disillusioned. They can see that feminism hasn't brought women the satisfaction it promised. Today's women are searching for answers. They want to know how to make life work.

Ultimately their longing will only be satisfied by embracing the gospel of Jesus Christ and a biblical understanding of manhood, womanhood, and gender relationships. The time is ripe for a new movement—a seismic, holy quake of countercultural Christian women who dare to take God at His Word, who have the courage to stand against the popular tide, choosing to believe and delight in God's plan for male and female.

And I say we get ready to take it "a long way, baby."

*This address, delivered at True Woman '08, is based on* The Feminist Mistake *by Mary A. Kassian (Wheaton, Illinois: Crossway Books, 2005) and contains select quotations from that work. Used by permission.*

# for such a time
# **as this**

## NANCY LEIGH DeMOSS

Not long ago, I was studying in a condo overlooking Lake Michigan, the gracious gift of a friend who had invited me to stay there as I worked. On this particular day, the sky was unusually dark and dreary, with rain falling steadily throughout the day, making the mood even more dismal. Then, shortly before dusk, the rain subsided. In the western sky, a shaft of sunlight began to burn its way through the heavy, low-lying clouds, glimmering on the surface of the water.

Over the next few minutes, I watched as the sun burst through the dark clouds in a glorious display of light. Even though much of the early evening sky remained dark and foreboding, the window opened by the sun's rays and the beautiful sunset that followed were a picture to me of what I believe God wants to do in our day.

Spiritually speaking, the weather outside is dark and dreary—with signs of even more rain in the forecast. There are many days when it is difficult to see evidence of God's presence in our land and perhaps even in our own lives.

But beyond the clouds, beyond the darkness, God's rule and reign is as sure as the morning. Conditions may seem hard and cold and steely gray at the moment, but the One who made the heavens and the earth lives forever. And He will have the final word.

> *In all of life, it's important to recognize that there are always two stories going on at the same time.*

As I sat there that evening and watched the setting sun dominating the clouds, I found myself praying, "Oh Lord, may Your glory and the light of Your presence shine through my life and through Your people and dispel the darkness in our land." I believe God desires and is able to do just that!

## Two Stories . . . Two Kingdoms

The dramatic events recorded in the book of Esther took place roughly 2,500 years ago, at a particularly dark moment in Israel's history, a period not unlike our own in many respects. But as ominous as Esther's era had become, the biblical account that bears her name tells of God pulling back the curtain, displaying His glory in the midst of an unholy world, and using a young woman in a significant way as an instrument of His redeeming work.

It's a "true woman" story.

In all of life, it's important to recognize that there are always two stories going on at the same time—two perspectives, two worldviews, two ways of looking at life. There's the drama that you can see, and then there's the drama *behind* the drama. There's the obvious plot, as well as the plot *beneath* the plot.

The first plot is the visible, human one—the drama taking place on earth. We might call this the *kingdom of man*, as described, for example, in the first chapter of Esther when "in the days of Ahasuerus," we see the Persian king seated on his royal throne, hosting a feast for all his officials and servants, showing off "the riches of his royal glory and the splendor and pomp of his greatness for many days" (1:2, 4). This is the obvious story, the scene everyone in the room could witness. It's the story taking place in the natural, physical realm, the one that often seems to be the most powerful and impressive.

The kingdom of man is built on a foundation of self; it showcases the glory of man, as this ancient king sought to do. But Ahasuerus was building for himself a house of cards, as most people in the world are doing today.

You see, the natural, visible story is not the ultimate story. Backlighting the human plot and story is a heavenly drama, an unseen story that's always going on behind the scenes in the spiritual realm. It is the *Kingdom of God*, overshadowing and outdistancing the kingdom of man as God fulfills His eternal purposes through the events on earth.

This is what we see happening in the book of Esther, which in many ways is not her story at all. The leading character—as always—is God, whose name is never even mentioned, but whose presence and power are indisputable. And so it is in our own lives. The kingdom of man is clearly visible all about us. We can give it names and faces and GPS locations. But the kingdom of man is fleeting and frail and destined for destruction. Life on this earth is merely a vapor. One day it will dissipate and be replaced by a greater reality.

Therefore, we as true women, playing out our individual roles in the story of our times, must keep our eyes on what is unseen, knowing that what our God is doing in the background is higher, broader, and more eternal than anything we can see with our natural sight.

Like Esther, we too have been placed in our world "for such a time as this," for the honor and glory of our Father. And we, like she, must live in light of that calling, giving this world a vision of His reality, power, and grace.

## Setting the Stage

The Bible tells us that Ahasuerus "reigned from India to Ethiopia over 127 provinces" (1:1)—the highest throne on earth at the time. And the grand gathering depicted in the first chapter of Esther is certainly indicative of his place in world events. "The army of Persia and Media and the nobles and governors of the provinces were before him" (v. 3). We see a picture of massive, opulent wealth. Pomp, circumstance, and influence. The gala celebration could hardly have been more festive. Day after day, from room to royal room—feasting, partying, celebrating. It's a splendid portrait of the greatness of man.

Ahasuerus is on his high and lifted-up throne, thinking he is the king of the world, but all the while God is on His holy throne in heaven, seated far above all earthly kings. History describes Ahasuerus as a godless, ruthless man. In his arrogance, he thought he ran the world and answered to no one, but the unseen hand of God was in control, moving and working behind the scenes to accomplish His purposes.

You're likely familiar with what happened on the seventh day of his feast when, drunk and feeling especially domineering, he ordered Queen Vashti to appear before the assembled crowd to show off her beauty (actually, to show off what kind of beauty he had been able to conquer for himself). Vashti refused to respond to the king's summons and found herself summarily deposed as a result.

Fast-forward four years, and you arrive at chapter two, the king having returned from a consuming campaign in Greece. Recalling that he was in the market for a new queen, he began the official process for finding Vashti's replacement.

And this is where we're introduced to a Jewish girl named Esther.

## Esther's Rise

Both of Esther's parents had died, and she was being raised by an older cousin, Mordecai. But through a series of circumstances, she was taken into the king's harem and custody in the palace. Providentially, everywhere she went, "Esther was winning favor in the eyes of all who saw her" (2:15). In fact, "the king loved Esther more than all the women, and she won grace and favor in his sight more than all the virgins, so that he had set the royal crown on her head and made her queen instead of Vashti" (v. 17).

Yes, a Jewess had been crowned the First Lady of Persia, her nationality unknown even to the king himself.

Remember: one book, two stories. Like always.

From the perspective of the human drama—the kingdom of man—Esther's rise to Persian prominence could be considered a notable accomplishment, a huge boost to her self-esteem, a reason for great pride. She had gone from nobody to queen in short order, an enviable career path in the eyes of some.

Of course, you could also look at it another way, even from the kingdom-of-man perspective. Being married to an angry, arrogant, unbelieving man, even if he happened to be king, would not be a position most of us would envy. You could feel quite sorry for her. Her family had been carried away from their homeland. She had been orphaned. Her "fate"—a word that's used often in the human drama

> **"What is God up to?"**
> *That's what really matters.*

of events—had put her in a bad situation that was likely to get nothing but worse. Kings with the authority and access to any female they want are not disposed to being faithful husbands. We know how things turned out for Vashti when *she* quit being pleasing to her husband.

But looking at this story in terms of the Kingdom of God, we no longer think of it as a rags-to-riches fairy tale, nor do we bemoan her fate, determining that she's gotten a bum deal. Those kinds of judgments and analyses are not the currency of the Kingdom of God.

Instead, we view this entire turn of events through a much larger lens, a much wider scope. And we see that this story is really about God and *His* agenda, God and *His* aims, God and *His* purposes.

*"What is God up to?"* That's what really matters.

Esther is not the star but simply a player in the heavenly drama being acted out on an earthly stage. Ultimately it was God who raised her to this lofty position in a pagan land. It was God who put her in the palace of a wicked king. She had been placed here by God for Kingdom purposes which—note this—were totally unknown to her.

I want to remind you that you, too, have been positioned by God in *your* place right now for His own Kingdom purposes. You may say, "My circumstances are not to my liking." God understands that. He knows exactly what you're dealing with. But He is accomplishing the goals of His heavenly drama through you, purposes that are bigger and more eternal than anything you can see or understand. His plans are sure. He is in total control.

So whether you win or lose the world's beauty and popularity contests, whether you land your dream job or lose the one you've got, whether you're financially prosperous or watching years of accumulated earnings lose their value, whether you have healthy children or a child with special needs, whether you have an intact family background or a dysfunctional one, whether you're physically fit or struggling with sickness—these things matter greatly in the kingdom of man, but they pale into insignificance in the Kingdom of God.

The question is not, "How will this circumstance affect me?" or, "How will it fulfill my wants and needs?" The right question to ask is, "How does God want to use my position, my season of life, my place at this moment in time to fulfill His Kingdom purposes in the world?"

## Living under Providence

Remember, there are no "chance" circumstances in our lives, nor in the world at large. Even details that seem trivial and insignificant are part of God's divine plan and process. He is always at work. All we can see is here and now and this isolated moment, but God sees the entire eternal span of the picture. That's why we can trust Him.

In the human drama, some of the circumstances we go through seem to make no sense at all. They seem completely unfair. Take, for example, the "happenings" in the life of Mordecai, Esther's older cousin who had taken her under his wing. He was a humble servant, a man of honor and character. But when he uncovered and exposed a plot to assassinate the king, he went unrewarded and misunderstood . . . for a while. Taking a time stamp from that particular point in his story, he would have had reason to grouse and complain—just as we undoubtedly would be tempted to do if put in the same position.

We've all been there—in the center of an injustice, hemmed in by the details of our current situation, basing our reactions on a single snapshot of this unfair moment in time. But we need to train ourselves, deny ourselves, humble ourselves enough to say, "Lord, from my limited view, this doesn't make sense. But I know You see the bigger picture, and I trust You."

So humble, loyal Mordecai goes unrewarded. On the other hand, Haman, who is a proud, vicious, conniving man, is promoted to chief of staff and everyone bows down to him. Doesn't seem fair, does it? But remember, this is just the visible story on the human level. And it's just for a moment, when seen against the backdrop of eternity. Remember that God is going to right all wrongs. Wait on the Lord; be patient; He will act—in His way and His time.

## Kingdoms in Conflict

Meanwhile, Haman becomes angry when he notices Mordecai refusing to bow and give him the homage his new title deserves. So taking the opportunity to wreak his revenge, Haman uses his position with the king to propose an edict that would authorize the extermination of the Jews, backed up by ten thousand talents of silver he offers to pay into the royal coffers himself. The king goes along with this suggestion, being persuaded by Haman that "it [is] not to the king's profit to tolerate" this people with their strange customs and their own laws (3:8).

So letters are sent out by courier to all the king's provinces, giving instructions to kill all the Jews—young and old, women and children—in one day on the calendar, the thirteenth day of Adar. Then we read, "The king and Haman sat down to drink, but the city of Susa [the capital city] was thrown into confusion" (v. 15).

We know about cities being "thrown into confusion." We've seen what happens when news reports begin to break, announcing the potential of a gas shortage or the impending bankruptcy of a major employer. "All Signs Pointing to Panic"—I remember seeing the headline blaring on the front page of the *Chicago Tribune* at the outset of the economic collapse in the fall of 2008. That's often the mood in the kingdom of man—panic, anxiety, apprehension, fear, dread—"confusion." But there's never an iota of confusion in the Kingdom of God. Only plans—God's wise, good, eternal plans.

Upon hearing news of the king's death order, Mordecai reacted as all men and women of God should act when the wicked prevail and things become desperate. Rather than striking back and demanding justice from men, he cried out "with a loud and bitter cry" to God (4:1). "And in every province, wherever the king's command and his decree reached, there was great mourning among the Jews, with fasting and weeping and lamenting, and many of them lay in sackcloth and ashes" (v. 3).

> *How often do we see a spirit of mourning, fasting, and humility in our churches or in this land?*

We have a National Day of Prayer in America, an annual event that became part of established law during the Truman administration, and was later amended by President Ronald Reagan to be conducted on the first Thursday of every May. However, in the past, as at the height of the Civil War in 1863 during the presidency of Abraham Lincoln, our nation observed not just days of prayer, but days of "humiliation, fasting, and prayer."

Those are the kinds of prayer gatherings we need to call for today—periods of donning spiritual sackcloth and ashes. Yet how often do we see a spirit of mourning, fasting, and humility in our churches or in this land? The fact that we don't see that kind of outpouring today indicates to me that we're not yet desperate enough, not yet convinced that we can't get out of these messes ourselves, not yet sure that the Kingdom of God has the only answer for what ails us. Mordecai and the Jews of Esther's day had nowhere else to turn but to the Lord.

And when Queen Esther, closeted away in the palace, heard of the turmoil and unrest in the streets, she sent out one of her attendants, Hathach, to find out what was going on. He went first to Mordecai, still distressed and in ashes at the king's gate, where Mordecai told him everything that had happened, giving him a written copy of the decree to take to Esther that she might "go to the king to beg his favor and plead with him on behalf of her people" (v. 8).

But what could she really do about it? As she tried to explain to Mordecai by way of Hathach, "If any man or woman goes to the king inside the inner court without being called, there is but one law—to be put to death, except the one to whom the king holds out the golden scepter so that he may live" (v. 11). Besides, it had been more than a month, she said, since she had even seen the king.

"You are sending me on a suicide mission!" Esther was trying to say. "What good can I do *anyone* if my attempt to help leads to my death?"

## A Crisis of Faith

Then we come to the heart of Esther's story—the sliver of light cutting through the darkest of dark clouds, where the kingdom of man is illuminated by the backlight of the Kingdom of God. Mordecai said:

*Do not think to yourself that in the king's palace you will escape any more than all the other Jews. For if you keep silent at this time, relief and deliverance will rise for the Jews from another place, but you and your father's house will perish. And who knows whether you have not come to the kingdom for such a time as this?* (vv. 13–14)

Mordecai is saying in effect, "God is not dependent on you. He doesn't need you to accomplish His purposes. God will win with or without you and me. He can bring deliverance from other sources. But," he reminds Esther, "there are a lot of lives at stake—you, your family, your people."

And then those familiar words: *"Who knows whether you have not come to the kingdom for such a time as this?"*

Whether it was Esther then or you today, only God knows—and only time will tell—why He has sovereignly placed you where you are right now, at this moment in history. You have been given a role to play, and no one else can fill it.

You say, "Look, Nancy, I'm not a speaker. I don't lead anything. I don't have any interesting gifts or talents or abilities." That may all be true. But the fact remains that you are not here by accident. Whatever your season of life, your marital status, your vocation, your natural gifting, you have been given privileges, opportunities, and a place in the kingdom—the kingdom of man—at this time, to be used to further the Kingdom of God.

When Mordecai's words reached Esther's ears, she realized what she must do. The excuses she had made, the fears she had harbored, all the human rationales she had concocted for hesitating to step into her God-designed role—all of it was overcome as the truth swept over her spirit. She knew there was no time for delay and that she must take decisive action. So she sent back word to Mordecai:

> *Go, gather all the Jews to be found in Susa, and hold a fast on my behalf, and do not eat or drink for three days, night or day. I and my young women will also fast as you do. Then I will go to the king, though it is against the law, and if I perish, I perish.* (v. 16)

Notice that she didn't act alone. She realized she was part of a community; she understood the necessity of being in one accord. There's a reminder here of the importance of linking hearts and hands with other believers as we seek to deal with the issues in our day that oppose the Kingdom of God.

We also see a sense of urgency that prompts Esther to call for a three-day fast. Drastic days call for drastic measures. This was no time to play Trivial Pursuit. Before attempting to stand before the king of Persia, it was imperative that she first go before the King of the universe, the One who lifts up kings and brings them down. Fasting and prayer were not ends in themselves. They were preparing her heart, preparing the way for her to move forward with God's intervening blessing on her behalf and on behalf of her people.

So she says in verse 16, "I will go to the king, though it is against the law, and if I perish, I perish." Here's a woman who is going for broke. This is not a half-hearted effort; it's not a half-hearted commitment. She lays everything on the line in order to fulfill God's calling for her life—even if it means giving up her life.

As I was studying this text, I happened quite providentially on a message by Dr. Tim Keller, senior pastor of Redeemer Presbyterian Church in New York City, in which he made a passing comment about Esther that has stuck with me. He pointed out that Esther, in taking her bold measure of faith, was willing to leave the palace, risking her life in order to save her people. The Lord Jesus, by comparison, actually *did* leave His heavenly palace, giving up His life in order to save His people. In this way, Esther's story foreshadows the gospel message, even as our lives are intended to point people to the redeeming heart and work of Christ.

> *You too are a tool in the hand of God.*

As you know, God supernaturally intervened in the life of Esther. The Jews were spared from annihilation. Haman was exposed and brought to justice. Mordecai was exalted. Thus, we have an important chapter in the history of redemption—a kingdom-of-man moment transformed into a Kingdom of God moment by (who else?) God Himself.

And though you may not view your life as ranking anywhere near the level of importance with Esther, this is not the way your Father sees it. You too are a tool in the hand of God, being applied to situations that may just feel like "everyday life" to you but are actually backlit stages where the purposes of God are being put on display from your street address. And He knows the audience He's playing to, whether it be members of your family, church friends, random acquaintances—whoever needs to see His power at work in a surrendered heart . . . like yours.

## Perspective and Hope for the Battle

So as we consider what it means for us to be true women of God in our day, I want to suggest several important insights and lessons we can glean from the story of Esther.

**1) *We are in a battle.*** We know that Haman's corrupt counsel to the king was inspired by Satan, who was determined to wipe out the line of Christ. This archenemy of God was threatening the continuity of God's purposes in redemptive history, threatening the future existence of God's chosen people, threatening the appearance of the Messiah. The battle was not really between Haman and Mordecai. Though they were real people making real choices in a real world, they were more like pawns on a chessboard, symbols of a conflict between the kingdom of man (pledging allegiance to Satan) and the Kingdom of God.

We need to remember that our battle as true women today is not against human powers or political parties or secular culture. Our battle is not against those who promote feminist ideologies. It's not fundamentally against men who mistreat or belittle women. None of these is the ultimate enemy. The battle we are waging is a *spiritual* battle, and we need to keep our eyes on that reality.

**2) *The weapons and tactics of the earthly, human kingdom are different than the weapons and tactics of the heavenly Kingdom.*** In the human drama, men depend on weapons like worldly power, human laws and decrees, military might, self-sufficiency, anger, force, and deception to accomplish their ends and advance their cause. The children of the Kingdom of God fight and win the war with humility, prayer, fasting, truth, and love, relying on God to go before them and fight their battles. That is not to say that we should not attempt to use legal and political means to affect societal change and protect the oppressed. But we must recognize that the bigger battle is fought on a different, higher plane.

When you feel caught in the fray, remember that "the battle is not yours but God's" (2 Chronicles 20:15), and that regardless of the outcome of elections, the economy, or anything involved in your personal situation—marital crisis, family problems, physical sickness, church, relational, and cultural issues—the real battle is fought and won in the spiritual realm with spiritual weapons and tactics.

**3) *God has a sovereign, redemptive plan, and it will not fail.*** He has a plan for your life, for your family, for His people, and for this world—a plan to reveal the glory and splendor of the saving grace of Jesus Christ, filling the earth with His glory. And no matter what happens in the halls of government, the financial markets, or the corporate board rooms, His plan will not fail. No ungodly husband can thwart it. No prodigal child can derail it. No depth of sadness, regret, or depression can delay it. Nothing in this world can abort His eternal plan. Even when you cannot see His hand, even when it seems that nothing is happening, God is always behind the scenes fulfilling His purposes. He will prevail.

**4) *Through faith and obedience, you can be part of God's plan.*** There may be times when you feel alone in this battle, times when you feel helpless and outnumbered, overwhelmed by ungodliness and the powers of darkness. But never underestimate the power of God. Never underestimate the significance and influence of your faith, your prayers, your faithfulness, and your obedience. Don't think your life can't make a difference. The potential impact of one woman who is filled with the Spirit of God and is available for His Kingdom purposes is incalculable. Just look at Esther—and Mary, and Sarah, and Ruth, and Deborah—real-life sisters of another age.

Young or old, outgoing or subdued, healthy or frail, God has brought you into His Kingdom "for such a time as this." So be courageous. Be willing to step out in faith. Be ready for Him to use you as He desires, to accomplish His eternal purposes in your world.

**5) *No situation is so desperate that God cannot redeem it.*** If ever there was a situation that seemed hopeless, it was Esther's. Orphaned as a girl; taken into a Persian harem, married to a cruel, arrogant, alcoholic husband; then faced with an edict intended to exterminate her entire race. It was a desperate situation, both for her and for her people. Her plight seemed hopeless. But the heavenly Kingdom rules over the earthly kingdom.

When we are in the midst of that earthly drama, facing dire circumstances, we must keep reminding ourselves of this ultimate reality: *Heaven rules!* Remember what Pastor John Piper said? "In every situation and circumstance of your life, God is always doing a thousand different things that you cannot see and you do not know." Never forget that. Write it on the tablet of your heart. And learn to wait for God to act, to wait on His time. The fact is, all the pushing, nagging, screaming, yelling, badgering, manipulating, whining, and shaming in the world won't solve your problems. Those tactics may help you get your way in an immediate sense, but they will not win victories for the Kingdom of God. Making things happen is *His* role in your situation, and He is sure to act in His perfect time, according to His good, sovereign, and eternal will. It will be worth the wait, I assure you.

We tend to justify our impatient behavior, becoming shrews and getting shrill when our circumstances become the most dire or distasteful. But anger and ugliness should not characterize our reactions to injustices and painful situations, whether in dealing with issues in the public square or personal matters. Even when called to confront evil, true women are marked by a spirit of grace and meekness. They keep their power under control—under *God's* control.

Faced with a diabolical scheme that threatened her life along with her entire Jewish race, Esther was a woman who stayed remarkably in control of her tongue and her emotions. No hurry, no histrionics, no hysterical outbursts. Her example provides a portrait of a woman who acted as if she understood that the Kingdom of God was in control. And because heaven rules, *we* can respond to even the most threatening circumstances with courage, faith, and quiet confidence.

**6)** *Don't judge the outcome of the battle by the way things look right now.* As we saw with Mordecai and Haman, in this world the wicked often flourish and the godly often suffer. At various points in Esther's story, the wicked are partying and the righteous are mourning. But by the close of the book, the wicked have been judged and the righteous are partying. That is a glimpse of our future hope.

Remember that things are not now as they will always be. Yes, the wicked and unjust may be riding high in your life right now, but judgment is coming one day, and they will have to give an account. The righteous may suffer now, but one day they will share in the eternal triumph in the Kingdom of God. The Man riding on a white horse will come to take over, bursting through the clouds for all the world to see. Then there will be everlasting joy for the people of God, bought by the blood of His Son. "Surely there is a reward for the righteous; surely there is a God who judges on earth" (Psalm 58:11). God will get the last word and write the final chapter.

In fact, the final chapter has already been written. It's not as though God is sitting up in heaven, saying, "Oh my, what in the world am I going to do about all of these crises taking place down there? How am I going to solve all these problems?" Oh my sister, there are no mysteries in heaven as there are on earth. The entire story, from first to final chapter, was written by God in eternity past; it is being unfolded in our present day, waiting for its ultimate outworking in eternity future.

See with the eyes of faith. Live in the hope of God's sure and certain promises.

## Against the Tide

Our hearts' desire, as true women, is for the Kingdom of God to be established and evident in our lives and for Christ to be exalted and reign supreme in our world.

Yet, much as you may resonate with this vision, it may seem way out of touch with reality. From where you sit today, you may feel very alone and inadequate to live out, much less champion, a mission so radically contrary to the established world system. You may imagine what some of your girlfriends would say if you talked about how important it is to live by these biblical truths, to be so secure and surrendered to the Lord that you can embrace your problems under the umbrella of His sovereignty. You may wonder, once you put this book away, whether this whole True Woman mind-set is realistic or relevant for our day. What difference does it make what Christian women do in a world that already thinks we're nuts because we don't talk the way they do, don't sleep around the way they do, don't possess the same attitudes as they do?

Well, what difference did it make for Esther to live as a true woman of God? She was a common, ordinary young woman, caught up in the human drama of her day, faced with challenges that could easily have kept her from becoming a woman of courage and faith. But as a result of her surrender and obedience, millions of people were spared from destruction.

A once-in-a-millennium event, you say? A story from another time that is far removed from the life you lead and the day in which we live?

Please believe me when I say that the wondrous acts of God are not limited to by-gone days. Our powerful, redeeming God is alive; He has not abdicated His throne; He is intent on displaying His glory in our world. And our minds cannot fathom all that He is able to do in and through the lives of those who trust Him.

> *Oh, how abundant is your goodness,*
> *which you have stored up for those who fear you*
> *and worked for those who take refuge in you,*
> *in the sight of the children of mankind!* (Psalm 31:19)

*Oh, Father, may we hear and heed Your call. Make us Your true women—for Jesus' sake, and for the sake of Your great Kingdom. Amen.*

# PART THREE

# the refining of
# true womanhood

*We are called to be women.*
*The fact that I am a woman does not make me a different kind of Christian,*
*but the fact that I am a Christian does make me a different kind of woman.*
*For I have accepted God's idea of me,*
*and my whole life is an offering back to Him*
*of all that I am and all that He wants me to be.*[1]

—ELISABETH ELLIOT

# a woman after God's
# **own heart**

## JANET PARSHALL

My husband, Craig, and I once lived in Fredericksburg, Virginia, the place where George Washington also lived many years earlier from the age of seven to twenty-one. If he ever threw a silver dollar across the river, it certainly wasn't across the Potomac, as the legend goes. It was across the river in Fredericksburg called the Rappahannock. But more significant than the Rappahannock River in the young life of George Washington was another Fredericksburg landmark that played forcefully into his future—a small jetty of rock not far from where his mother is now buried.

Many prayers ascended heavenward from that place. His mother was known to walk out to that rock on frequent occasions, praying for her family, praying for her children, praying for George. Biographers have left us story after story of the great General Washington, locked in the heat of battle, being preserved by God's gracious answers to the effectual prayers of a mother, praying ceaselessly for her son.

Washington said, "My mother was the most beautiful woman I ever saw, and all I am I owe to my mother. I attribute all my successes to the moral, intellectual, and physical education I received from her." It's amazing, the power of a praying mother.

Abraham Lincoln, too, had much to say about his mother, including this touching tribute to her influence on the man he became: "I remember my mother's prayers, and they have always followed me. They have clung with me all my life."

So can the prayers of a praying woman affect the course of a nation?

Let's consider the answer—as well as a number of other discoveries about the role of women in God's Kingdom purposes—through a familiar Bible story about a true woman of faith.

## An Ancient Ordeal

The condition of ancient Israel could hardly have been worse than during the period of the Judges, when not once, but twice (Judges 17:6; 21:25), the Scripture reveals, "In those days there was no king in Israel. Everyone did what was right in his own eyes." Israel had no leader. She had a defiled priesthood. The country was in absolute disarray. But in the midst of all this cultural chaos and hopelessness comes an amazing story—a mother who lifts up her heartbreak to the One who knows how to heal it.

No matter how many times you've heard this story, the Word remains living and vibrant. Whenever you drop down that plumb line, you pull up a new truth. So even if you've heard it a thousand times, may you discover something new about this precious woman. And if perhaps the story is new to you, prepare to be introduced to a truly magnificent woman of faith.

The situation begins this way:

> *There was a certain man of Ramathaim-zophim of the hill country of Ephraim whose name was Elkanah the son of Jeroham, son of Elihu, son of Tohu, son of Zuph, an Ephrathite. He had two wives. The name of the one was Hannah, and the name of the other, Peninnah. And Peninnah had children, but Hannah had no children.* (1 Samuel 1:1–2)

We're only two verses into this pivotal account from Israel's history, and already we have some problems. First of all, we see one too many wives.

One of the recurring scenes of the Old Testament is the presence of polygamy and the discord it created. Go through the Scriptures and you'll see that Abraham had two wives—and problems. Jacob had two wives—and problems. Both David and Solomon had multiple wives—and all kinds of resulting problems. So although it was not God's created ideal, He obviously allowed His people to choose polygamy. But every time polygamy was practiced in the Bible, it brought trouble into the family's life.

I've heard people who advocate variations on the traditional form of marriage say, "Well, even your Bible talks about polygamy," to which I'm quick to say, "Oh, yes, it does, but you need to read the rest of the story. Because every time there's polygamy, there's a problem." Whenever a society begins to tinker with the institution of marriage, created by God in a perfect environment called Eden, we are undermining a profound and precious gift—whether in the ancient Near East or in the time and place we call our own.

So as we watch what happens in states that are legislating and voting on changes to traditional marriage, we must recognize that God's truth is at stake. In the end, this is not a political issue; it is a biblical issue. When state supreme courts begin ruling that same-sex marriages are to be legalized and officially recognized, we are striking at the heart of God's good and perfect plan, and we inherit the whirlwind as a result.

The other issue introduced in the opening two verses of 1 Samuel is that one of the two wives has children, and one does not. Many biblical scholars feel that perhaps Elkanah married Hannah first. But because she couldn't produce an heir, he then married Peninnah, who was able to bear multiple children. This situation clearly was causing deep tension between the two women.

*Now this man used to go up year by year from his city to worship and to sacrifice to the Lord of hosts at Shiloh, where the two sons of Eli, Hophni and Phineas, were priests of the Lord. On the day when Elkanah sacrificed, he would give portions to Peninnah his wife and to all her sons and daughters. But to Hannah he gave a double portion, because he loved her, though the Lord had closed her womb.* (vv. 3–5)

It's obvious that Elkanah loved Hannah. After all, he gave her a double portion. Don't make little of this. It was his love letter to her, affirming her value in his life even though she hadn't provided him any children. The customs of the day gave him ample grounds to divorce her, for no other reason than that.

This mind-set can still be found in some parts of the world. Craig and I were recently in Cairo, dining with an Egyptologist in an Indian restaurant. It was like a scene from a Humphrey Bogart movie. This large Egyptian man went on and on about his wife who had given him two fine daughters, talking about how much he loved the two girls and how much he loved his wife. Stopping for breath and to take a slow drag off his cigarette, he blew a circle of smoke into the air, then looked at Craig and me, and said, "But it's time for me to get another wife."

I thought he was being facetious at first, so treading lightly, I said, "Why would you get a second wife?" To which he responded, "Because my first one hasn't given me any sons, and I need sons."

Insert Elkanah into this chauvinistic scenario. He easily could have gotten rid of Hannah for not creating a mandatory lineage for him, just as the twenty-first-century Egyptian man was planning to do in conjunction with Islamic law, which allows him to take up to *four* wives. In the cultural milieu of Elkanah's day, a woman's worth was predicated on her progeny. Hannah didn't produce; Peninnah did. Yet in the midst of this tense scenario, we see that Elkanah loved Hannah. He gave her a double portion.

Even more poignant to this scene, however, is the final statement of verse 5: "The Lord had closed her womb." Uh-oh. Now we have a sovereignty issue at work here. Could God actually make a woman infertile?

Oh, yes. That could be part of His good and perfect plan.

I know how hard it must be for some to read and ponder this. But what if it is God's perfect plan that a woman never has children? Does it make Him a puny God? Does it make Him insufficient and uncaring? Or is He still the sovereign Lord of all?

"The Lord had closed her womb." Scripture says it as plainly as that. But don't doubt for one minute that He had a reason and purpose for this. This was God, acting in His sovereignty, performing His work in ways that were inscrutable to this wife whose hopes and longings remained unfulfilled month after month.

> *What if it is God's perfect plan that a woman never has children? Does it make Him a puny God?*

Can you accept His will for your life right now, even if it's not what you want? Perhaps you desperately want to be married, but God says . . . no. Perhaps you desperately want children, but God says . . . no. Perhaps you desperately want your husband healed of sickness or some other troubling condition, but God says . . . no.

Does this make you doubt His love for you? Do you start saying to Him, "I can't trust You"? If your answer is yes . . . why? Because He's not the ATM of every prayer request? Because He doesn't give us what we always want? Because in our boastful nature we presume to know what is best for us? If everything that comes into our lives is filtered through the grid of His wisdom, goodness, and love—and it is—can we trust Him? We so easily say, "Oh God, I love You," but how we balk at saying, "God, I also trust You."

## Drastic Measures

The other woman—Peninnah—was more than a pain in the neck to Hannah. Look at the title the Bible uses to describe her: "Her rival used to provoke her grievously to irritate her, because the Lord had closed her womb" (v. 6). Scripture doesn't tell us exactly how she "provoked" Hannah, but we can use our sanctified imaginations to get close to the answer.

Peninnah was a fertile woman with multiple sons and daughters, lording her abilities at childbearing over her infertile counterpart. Perhaps it went something like this: "Oh, Hannah, could you get me some water from the well? My legs are so swollen, and I've been dealing with leg cramps. You know how it is when you're pregnant—oh, that's right, you *don't* know how it is when you're pregnant."

> *Sometimes God allows obnoxious people into our lives, and when He does, He has His reasons.*

Catty women probably haven't changed much over the years. Oh, what it must have been like, year after year, having to share the same household with this woman!

What would your perspective have been? If it was God's good and perfect plan, yet here was this absolutely obnoxious and irritating person in your life who just wouldn't go away, would you say, "God, You're making a mistake"? Or would you perhaps be wondering what God was trying to squeeze out of you through this intolerable situation? Sometimes God allows obnoxious people into our lives, and when He does, He has His reasons. Those aren't lessons I'm entirely fond of, but I know He does it.

And it went on like this for Hannah "year by year. As often as she went up to the house of the Lord, [Peninnah] used to provoke her. Therefore Hannah wept and would not eat" (v. 7). You don't have to be a clinical psychologist to realize that Hannah was depressed. Have you ever been so upset that the idea of food was nauseating to you? Or wept so hard that you couldn't draw your breath? Then you know how Hannah felt as this "rival" of hers kept constantly driving her to the brink of depression.

"I don't want to eat. I can't stop crying. Oh God, when will it stop?" How could Hannah press on?

Elkanah, her husband, would say to her, "Hannah, why do you weep?

And why do you not eat? And why is your heart sad? Am I not more to you than ten sons?" (v. 8).

Good question. On the one hand, she must have loved her husband. And yet she couldn't help but feel conflicted. We know she lived in a household where maternity was her security, her reason for being alive in this particular culture. Not being able to produce a child was a matter of deep shame and loss of value.

You see this same struggle elsewhere in the Scripture. Rachel told Jacob that if she didn't have children, she would rather die. Zechariah's wife Elizabeth knew the disgraceful looks she got from people all around her. She thought maybe she'd done something to make God mad. In Luke we read that when John was born, Elizabeth knew that the Lord had taken away "[her] reproach among people" (Luke 1:25). Hannah herself, we know, thought her childlessness was a punishment from God. This was more than just an infertility problem; this was a validation issue. And she was not being validated.

So when Elkanah asked her that question—perhaps holding up both hands with all his fingers extended, wanting so badly to be as valuable to her as "ten sons," the big family she wasn't able to have—Hannah's answer was . . .

Oh, that's right. The Scripture doesn't tell us how she answered. All we know is that "after they had eaten and drunk in Shiloh, Hannah rose" (v. 9). She stood up. Why would the Bible take the time to tell us what her posture was?

I admit that I may be reading something extrabiblical into the text, so don't take this as gospel. But I think that somewhere between the spaces of these words, Hannah's standing up was equivalent to her saying, "This is it. I need to get to a place in my life where I've completely surrendered this to God. I've got to let go. So I'm setting out for the temple, and I'm laying this at the feet of God."

I have a feeling that "standing up" meant "I'm going to stand on my trust in You." It was more than the position of her body; it was the position of her heart. She was a woman who was "deeply distressed." So she went to the temple, "prayed to the Lord, and wept bitterly" (v. 10).

I'd be surprised if you don't know what it means to be "deeply distressed," if you can't recall times in your own life when you've "prayed to the Lord and wept bitterly." Perhaps you've tear-stained your pillow in the middle of the night. Perhaps you've said good-bye to someone, buried your face in your hands, and sobbed until you didn't think you could draw your breath. Perhaps you've stood in an empty house, slumped to the floor of your kitchen, and poured out your heart to God at a level of intensity only a grieving woman knows.

So when it comes to talking about Hannah's bitterness of soul, the force of her emotion is not lost on you. "God, I'm so beside myself, I can't take another step. I'm letting go of this burden because I can't carry it anymore. And I'm begging You, Lord—please reveal Yourself to me." This is something we all understand.

And I think our Abba Father loves these prayers. When we're at the place where all we can say is, "Daddy, just pick me up in Your everlasting arms and wrap Your love around me," we're finally in the place where God can really begin to do something special with us. Yes, He's the magnificent, awe-inspiring, holy, and righteous King. But one of the great mysteries of our faith is that He is still our Father—which, by the way, makes us princesses. I can live with that!

But notice something else. At the height of Hannah's desperation and emotion, "she vowed a vow" (v. 11a).

The Bible says a lot about the making of vows, and the one impression that comes through loud and clear when you take all the texts and teachings together is this: you don't mess with vows. If you make a vow, you'd better be serious about it. "Let your 'yes' be yes and your 'no' be no, so that you may not fall under condemnation" (James 5:12). Genesis 24 reveals that at least on some occasions, a man making a vow in Old Testament times would put his hand under the other man's thigh—a serious, sealing, unforgettable act indeed. Vows mean business.

And so did Hannah's:

*"Lord of hosts, if you will indeed look on the affliction of your servant and remember me and not forget your servant, but will give to your servant a son, then I will give him to the Lord all the days of his life, and no razor shall touch his head."* (v. 11)

Most of us might have cut off our prayer after the "give to your servant a son" part. That's the self-evident longing, is it not? But Hannah sealed her prayer by the making of a bold, impassioned vow—a promise that if God would remove the ridicule of her rival by giving Hannah a son, she would give him back to God.

Stop and let her words trickle down from your brain into your heart. Could you have prayed Hannah's prayer? Could you ask God for the one thing—the one, big, obvious thing—that you desire most from Him, then promise to turn right around and give it back to the One who gave it? How could she do that?

She could do it because she was God-centered, because her relationship with the living God said, "Lord, I will trust You. I can surrender myself to You. I so believe in Your provision, compassion, and care that if You give me a son, I will show You my love by giving him back to You." That is truly a magnificent prayer.

A prayer that could change the course of a nation.

## How Much, How Long Can Faith Endure?

Picture the temple of Hannah's day. It was not like the later temple in Jerusalem, which was an actual structure of wood, stone, and precious metals. When we read that "Eli the priest was sitting on the seat beside the doorpost of the temple of the Lord" (v. 9b), realize that in place of pillars and columns would likely have just been pieces of linen. So even with Hannah standing back in the place where the women were allowed to be, the wind blowing through the temple would have parted the hangings of material, making it easy for Eli to look out and see her as she prayed.

And what he saw was something others could have probably caught us all doing at various junctions of our lives—crying out to God, yet crying in absolute silence—our lips moving wordlessly as the plaintiveness of our hearts percolates from the inside. Sometimes we can't do more than mouth what we're wanting to say, too upset and fatigued even to put volume behind it as we stand before God's throne of grace.

But for all Eli knew, Hannah's silent crying made her look like a drunken woman. And he thought he'd go over and tell her so. "How long will you go on being drunk? Put away your wine from you" (v. 14).

Imagine how maddening this must have been to Hannah. All these years she'd been getting one dig after another from her "rival" and housemate, Peninnah. Now when she slips away to the house of God to take her case before the Lord, even His priest is accusatory and condescending to her. His very words—"How long will you go on being drunk?"—are scalding with slander. He doesn't see her as someone who's perhaps momentarily drunk, as though this is an out-of-the-ordinary experience. He makes the quantum assumption that she's an alcoholic, hardly fit to approach the Lord in prayer.

If he'd have said it to me, I would have been tempted to lunge at him with hands ready to do bodily harm. But Hannah? Her response proves the rightness of her heart, and was eloquent in ways that left even old Eli convinced of the genuineness of her faith.

"No, my lord, I am a woman troubled in spirit. I have drunk neither wine nor strong drink, but I have been pouring out my soul before the Lord" (v. 15). As liquor might be poured out of its vessel, she described the depth of her desperation as if she were pouring it out of her soul before the Lord. "Do not regard your servant as a worthless woman, for all along I have been speaking out of my great anxiety and vexation" (v. 16).

Having shown (as the Proverbs would later relate) that "a soft answer turns away wrath" (15:1), her gentle and gracious spirit evoked from Eli, not an apology, but at least encouraging words of promise: "Go in peace, and the God of Israel grant your petition that you have made to him"

(1 Samuel 1:17). It was believed in those days that when the priest made such a bold statement, one could receive it as being prophetic. She could leave that holy place with a pretty good idea that her prayer was going to be answered. So she "went her way and ate, and her face was no longer sad" (v. 18).

Now we can read the first chapter of 1 Samuel in five minutes or less. We get to see the beginning, the middle, and the end of the story before our coffee's even gotten cold. But the true story of Hannah's faith and trust can only be seen by watching this experience through her eyes, imagining the slow walk that led to the fulfillment of God's promise.

*They rose early in the morning and worshiped before the Lord; then they went back to their house at Ramah. And Elkanah knew Hannah his wife, and the Lord remembered her. And in due time Hannah conceived and bore a son.* (vv. 19–20)

"In due time." This probably indicates that Hannah didn't get pregnant right away. Her faith in God's provision was hardly a demand, telling Him that He'd better come through before the week was out. In the idea expressed by the old hymn, "Trust and Obey"—"for there's no other way"—Hannah was apparently left to walk out her belief in God's goodness through the rising and setting of some period of days. "In due time."

*Was the priest right?* Still trusting. *Will I ever conceive?* Still trusting. *Will I have the son I'm so desperate for?* Still trusting. *Oh, Peninnah, not today* . . . Still trusting.

And finally—"in due time"—God's answer came rushing through. "Hannah conceived and bore a son, and she called his name Samuel, for she said, 'I have asked for him from the Lord'" (v. 20).

Still trusting.

## Here and Back

Knowing this story as we do, we're well aware that this is not the end. This is not where the lights come up and the credits roll. She had wanted this baby boy more desperately than she could put into words. He had been turning under her heart—kicking and rolling and getting the hic-cups. She now had the same leg cramps that Peninnah had perhaps always complained of.

But every little thump, kick, and movement had given rise to a quiet prayer of another kind, when she had forced herself to say—still trusting—"I have asked for him from the Lord. Yes, Lord, he's Yours."

It's not as though Hannah would be required to relinquish him one time only—on that fast approaching day when she would drop him off with Eli and walk away with the hard, lonely consequences of her vow. No, she had to relinquish her little prayed-for Samuel over and over and over again.

This reminds us of a profound reality: our children do not now—nor have they ever—belonged to us. They are God's. We are simply the happy participants in His lend-lease program. He gives us permission to touch their hearts and minds, to teach them, to write truth on the tablets of their life, to help them know the love of Christ their Savior, to inspire in them a love for God and His Word . . . and then they go. They're His, and His alone.

I'll never forget going to the door with Craig to answer an unexpected knock that came at 3:00 one morning, only to hear a police officer ask us, "Do you have a son named Sam?"

"Yes," we said, shock and raw adrenaline coursing through our answer.

"Your son's been shot in the head," the policeman told us, "and we don't know if he's dead or alive."

For three hours in the middle of the night, Craig and I drove through the Blue Ridge Mountains, knowing nothing else to do but to hold hands and quietly pray, with no way of knowing if our son was alive even at that moment. But somewhere in the quietude of that nightmarish car ride, I distinctly remember God gently reminding me, "Janet, you know he never did belong to you." And the only way I knew how to respond to Him was to answer back, "Thank You, Father God, that Sam knows You as Lord. If he's gone, he is now absent from the body and in Your presence. If he's not gone, You are the Great Physician, and You've already gone before us. So I praise You and thank You." It took hours. It wasn't easy. And it was all

God, not me. But by the time we reached our destination, I had loosened my grip on Sam's life. I realized he wasn't mine; he was His.

When he was born, I was fond of saying the words of Hannah over our own little Samuel: "For this child I prayed, and the Lord has granted me my petition that I made to him" (v. 27). How easy it was to pray this at the beginning of his young life. But what if I had to let go of him before I thought the time was right?

> *By the time we reached our destination, I had loosened my grip on Sam's life. I realized he wasn't mine; he was His.*

Thanks be to God, Sammy recovered after many long months of therapy and rehab. He's now married and has given us three darling grandchildren. Our God is indeed an awesome God. But I know a little of what Hannah felt. And even when we don't feel it—even when we forget that our children are His, not ours—the reality is true just the same.

Again, this relinquishing wasn't a one-time act on Hannah's part. As the Bible says:

> *The man Elkanah and all his house went up to offer to the Lord the yearly sacrifice and to pay his vow. But Hannah did not go up, for she said to her husband, "As soon as the child is weaned, I will bring him, so that he may appear in the presence of the Lord and dwell there forever." (vv. 21–22)*

The average weaning period for a child in Samuel's day was around three years of age. This meant that Hannah likely spent three whole years teaching him how to say his prayers, to tie his sandals, to make his little cot. She taught him how to fold his hands and give a blessing before he ate his food. She taught him how to worship at the temple, raised him in the nurture and admonition of the Lord. She caressed his little fevered brow when his first couple of teeth came in. She cradled him at night when he woke up frightened. She hugged him and rocked him at every opportunity. And every single day, she knew she was that much closer to giving him up for good.

Imagine how she sensed the loss during the intimacy of nursing him. God was aware how hard this would be on her as a mother. He later spoke these words through the prophet Isaiah: "Can a woman forget her nursing child, that she should have no compassion on the son of her womb? Even these may forget, yet I will not forget you" (Isaiah 49:15).

Here's the God of all creation—the One who came up with this idea of nursing babies, of creating that unbelievable bond and connectedness between mother and child—those moments when the baby falls asleep in your arms, you smell his sweet baby hair, and he curls his little fingers around yours. It's possible, the Scripture says, for a woman to forget some of what this feeling is like. But our great God declares that He will never forget. He knew what Hannah was going through.

But He also knew that she was a true woman. She was God-centered, not self-centered. She had a million reasons to say, "About that vow I made, God? I've changed my mind. I said it in a moment of frustration. I just can't go through with it now. He's become my boy. I'm not giving him up."

But that's not what Hannah did. She trusted God. "Lord, I don't know what the future holds, but I do know that You hold the future. You gave me this child, and I'm going to keep my vow. I'm giving him back to You, and he will be Yours all the days of his life."

She surrendered.

She said, "Yes, Lord."

And in so doing, she became a magnificent role model for the true woman.

*When she had weaned him, she took him up with her, along with a three-year-old bull, an ephah of flour, and a skin of wine and she brought him to the house of the Lord at Shiloh. And the child was young. Then they slaughtered the bull, and they brought the child to Eli. And she said, "Oh, my lord! As you live, my lord, I am the woman who was standing here in your presence, praying to the Lord. For this child I prayed, and the Lord has granted to me my petition that I made to him. Therefore I have lent him to the Lord. As long as he lives, he is lent to the Lord." (vv. 24–28)*

Further on in the narrative we read that "Samuel was ministering before the Lord, a boy clothed with a linen ephod. And his mother used to make him a little robe and take it to him each year when she went up with her husband to offer the yearly sacrifice" (2:18–19). The Bible could have been journalistic enough just to call it a robe, but the fact that God's inspired Word calls it a "little" robe reminds us as women that Samuel was still a small boy. Once a year his mother got to see him and bring him a little present. Can't you hear their conversation? "Oh, Samuel, how big you've gotten! Oh, Samuel, I never noticed how blue your eyes are. Oh, Samuel, do you remember me? Oh, Samuel, you belong to God."

When they turned to go back to Ramah, did she think to herself during the quiet journey back home, "One more year before I get to see him again"? Or did she think, "Oh, God, You're so gracious and kind. You gave me what I prayed for. What a joy to be able to turn right around and give him back to You." I think somehow it was probably the latter.

*Then Eli would bless Elkanah and his wife, and say, "May the Lord give you children by this woman for the petition she asked of the Lord." So then they would return to their home. Indeed the Lord visited Hannah, and she conceived and bore three sons and two daughters. And the young man Samuel grew in the presence of the Lord. (vv. 20–21)*

No, Hannah didn't know when she gave up her son that God would graciously fulfill her longing for children, but look how generous God is—exceedingly, abundantly beyond what we could ask for or imagine. "Hannah, do you trust Me? Hannah, are you willing to surrender to Me?" And God was faithful to fill her life with more blessings than her heart could hold.

## Prayers of a Mother

A wonderful parallel to Hannah's story is that of Moses' mother, Jochebed. Hiding her infant son from Pharaoh's wrathful decree until she could conceal him no longer, she put him in a basket and sent him down the Nile under daughter Miriam's watchful eye, entrusting her baby boy to the Lord's care and protection.

Pharaoh's daughter, you recall, just "happened" to be bathing nearby. Seeing the baby in the basket and desiring him for herself, she said, "I need someone to nurse this child." Miriam spoke up, saying something to the effect of, "I just happen to know a lactating Levite down the road a piece who can do the job!" So Jochebed got her baby back—but

> *Whether you have biological children or not, we are all spiritual mamas to somebody.*

only for a little while—those same three years that Hannah received to pour her heart and soul into her son and prepare him for the calling God had placed on his life.

The prayers of a mother. The prayers of Jochebed, praying for her son who would be used of God to deliver the Hebrews from bondage. The prayers of Hannah, praying for her son who would usher in a new age of righteousness and stability to the struggling, wandering nation of Israel. The prayers of Mary, praying for her Son who would not just change nations but truly change the world.

The prayers of a righteous mother truly avail much.

Whether you have biological children or not, we are all spiritual mamas to somebody. And we can all be praying—single women, women with a quiver full of children, women who've never borne children of their own. God has put us in the position of being true women of prayer for those He entrusts to our care. And when we're finally in glory, we'll be able to meet the ones we've been praying for so steadfastly.

Hannah's story teaches us what it means to be a true woman of God. She let go of her own plans. She knew that God was in charge, not her. She believed Him enough to say yes even when desperation had caused her to go out of her comfort zone and ask for the unthinkable.

Motherhood gives us feelings of fuzzy blankets and baby rattles and toys to line the crib. But motherhood is actually one of God's refining fires. The reality of motherhood is that it's a place to learn surrender, letting go, trusting and believing that God is God.

But because He is in it, motherhood gives us the opportunity to interact with history. Our prayers don't just become part of protecting our children from harm and from hazards of their own making. With God in control, our prayers for our children can make a mark on our nation. True women, like Hannah, trust God enough to believe He has great things planned for the babies He has given us—babies we give back to Him for His use, His Kingdom, His glory.

# choosing faith in seasons of
# **change**

## KAREN LORITTS

I had made up my mind. I wasn't going to let the empty nest surprise me. I was going to prepare for it. I was going to look forward to it. I was going to do this thing right.

Our last child was just entering high school, and with four years to go until our nest officially emptied, I thought I was well positioned to get my act together—ready to just be lovey-dovey with my man all over again, the way it was before the children came along. I'd heard all the war stories from my friends who had gone through menopause and the empty nest. Some of them said it was like some sort of disease creeping up on you. But I was too smart to let that happen. I was far enough out in front of the problem, with plenty of time to get good and ready for it.

This was going to be great. I just knew it.

Holly, our fourth, finally got to the point of graduating from high school. And like any mom who's preparing her child to go to college or into the work force or off to the military, I jumped in to help her get ready for the next phase of her life. My job that summer was to work on her dorm ensemble—the curtains, the bedspread, all the things a young college girl needs to get her new little "home" done up just the way she wants it.

We started in June, went through July, and finally came to August 14—the day we packed up all my baby girl's stuff into the SUV and drove her down to college to get started on her pre-med studies.

I'm not saying it was easy. We stayed down there a few days to help her get situated. We said our good-byes and cried a little. But I had been working four years to prepare myself for this. I didn't feel caught off guard. I had resolved to take on this challenge the way I'd taken on every challenge before.

Again, this was going to be fine. Great. I just knew it.

We returned home. September rolled around. I was cleaning up, organizing, making progress on things I'd been putting off for years. My plan seemed to be working. The house was quiet—just as I expected. The nest was empty—just as I knew it would be. Crawford and I had each other to ourselves again—just the way I'd pictured it.

Then came October 19. When a day like this hits, you don't round it up or down to the nearest ten or twenty. You don't group it into some general range of time, like "somewhere around the middle of the month." It was October 19.

And it was awful.

The day *started* fine and normal—what I'd call my *new* normal, after so many years of having children sprawled all over the house. I was sitting in my bedroom having my quiet time—sitting at the same chair, the same table, reading the same copy of the Bible. But the next thing I knew, tears were falling onto the pages. I hadn't even felt them coming. And as soon as I figured out what was happening, single tears had turned into a flood. I was sobbing. I couldn't stop. And I didn't know why. I just remember asking out loud, "Lord, what is happening to me?"

From out of nowhere, fear welled up in my belly as the torrent of tears continued to pour over the floodgates. Was it my time of the month? No. Crawford was out of town, but that had been our standard operating procedure for as long as I could remember. He was on staff with Campus

Crusade for Christ at the time and was usually gone from ten to fifteen days out of the month. It wasn't that.

It was so strange—as though the walls were talking to me, as though the house had finally quieted enough for me to really listen to the silence. And for the first time in a long, long time, I felt terribly alone. Terribly lonely. Then worry and fear began to wrap themselves around me like a garment. Despite all my hard work and preparation, I hadn't been able to fend off the one thing I was determined would not happen.

There was no other way to say it. I was having an emotional melt-down.

## Evil Companions

At the time of this unsettling event in my life, as well as the difficult few months that were to follow, I had been in ministry for more than thirty years. So an emotional meltdown was not something I thought a woman like me was supposed to have. And it took me a long time to come to grips with it and admit it.

Even though I didn't feel like getting out of the bed on some days, I didn't want to tell my husband what was happening to me. He's the kind of man who, out of his love for me and his desire to protect me, would want to fix it. I didn't really want him trying to fix this. I wanted to get out of it myself, with no one else knowing.

I kept trying to do all the right things in public, even in private. I kept praying. I kept up my speaking schedule. Crawford and I finished up a book on parenting we had been writing. But even with trying to press ahead and fulfill my duties, I could not shake this deep feeling in my bosom, a fear that was gripping me and refusing to let go.

But let me tell you something about fear. It doesn't usually come alone. It often brings along its buddies. And throughout the course of this downturn in my emotional strength, I identified at least ten little "fear buddies" that are prone to travel together when we're in the grasp of anxiety and loneliness. See if you haven't met up with some of these "fear buddies" yourself, and see if they haven't done some of these same kinds of things to you:

1) *Fear distorts reality.* One of the first thoughts I remember thinking when fear began descending around me was that, as of August 14 when I dropped off my youngest child at college, I wasn't a mother anymore. With three married adult children and one at school, I felt like my whole identity had walked away. Fear tries convincing you that things you know to be true are not exactly as they appear.

2) *Fear victimizes us.* It tries to beat you up. It dredges up all kinds of insecurities and inadequacies, then blows them all out of proportion. It makes you feel like you can't do anything well, even things that used to come quite naturally for you.

3) *Fear adds stress.* It affects you physically, emotionally, and spiritually, including symptoms such as high blood pressure, heartburn, and other stress-induced issues. You feel it all over.

4) *Fear creates doubt.* God was still with me during my emotional meltdown, but fear was tempting me to believe that He had abandoned me.

5) *Fear cripples us.* It immobilizes and paralyzes you. You feel stuck and incapable of making forward progress.

6) *Fear replaces faith.* During the time fear was tugging at me the most forcefully, I tended to forget that perfect love casts it out.

7) *Fear disappoints us.* It takes away more than it gives, leaving you nothing in return for all the worry and stress it causes.

8) *Fear makes us doubtful of success.* Not only does it draw you toward failure, it makes you fear moving ahead. It makes you wary and suspicious of any kind of improvement, doubting that any uptick in your perspective on life is either real or lasting.

9) *Fear fills our heart with despair.* It has a way of leaving you feeling utterly helpless and hopeless, unwilling to be consoled into believing the truth or hoping for a better day.

10) *Fear steals and destroys.* It makes you want to just walk off into a bottomless pit. Fear takes away your joy, victory, and blessing, leaving you empty and out of sorts.

## Fear Meets Its Match

With this kind of opposition around me, I knew I was in big trouble. But I knew I needed to get out of that bed, needed to believe God and trust Him with every single fiber of my being. I knew I couldn't let this despondent, defeated feeling become my new way of greeting each morning and facing each challenge. So one day—even though I didn't really feel like doing it yet—I pulled my Bible from its familiar place and read some things I had long known about but had strangely forgotten in the midst of my fear.

- *"The Lord is my light and my salvation; whom shall I fear? The Lord is the stronghold of my life; of whom shall I be afraid? . . . Though an enemy encamp against me, my heart shall not fear; though war arise against me, yet I will be confident"* (Psalm 27:1, 3).

- *"Do not be anxious about anything, but in everything by prayer and supplication with thanksgiving let your requests be made known to God"* (Philippians 4:6)—or as we might paraphrase it, "Bring your fears to God."

- *"Fear not, for I am with you; be not dismayed, for I am your God; I will strengthen you, I will help you, I will uphold you with my righteous right hand"* (Isaiah 41:10).

- With the children of Israel hemmed in by mountains and sea and an Egyptian army pursuing them from behind, Moses said to them above the commotion, *"The Lord will fight for you, and you have only to be silent"* (Exodus 14:14). Stand still and see the power of God working for you!

So that's what I did. I told God I would shut my mouth, that there was nothing more I could say. Enough was enough. No more would I allow fear to grip and rob me of my joy and blessing. Instead, I resolved three things to the Lord:

1) *I promise that I won't embarrass You.* I will not let fear cause me to act, speak, or imply anything that brings dishonor on Your name or on Your power to deliver Your people from bondage.

2) *I promise that I won't embarrass my husband.* I made a vow on May 22, 1971, that I would love, honor, and obey this man in sickness and in health, for richer or for poorer. I made a vow to love him, no matter what—whether hormones, PMS, empty nest, or whatever. I'm going to love my man the way You want me to love him.

3) *I promise that I won't embarrass myself.* I know too much about You, Lord, and the lengths You went to save me. I will not let fear lead me to debase and diminish the work You've done to get me this far.

Truly, I was one who shouldn't have been high on God's radar screen. I was born to an unwed teenage girl in the concrete jungle of Philadelphia. My mother had a brief affair with an older man and got pregnant as a result, but didn't want to marry him. After me came two others, all three of us with different fathers. So throughout my growing-up years, we were in and out of our grandmother's home, our auntie's home, anyone who would help my mom survive as a single parent.

By the age of ten, I was practically raising my two younger brothers. I was a lost puppy, looking for love and acceptance but finding nothing but hopelessness and despair. I decided at one point to kill myself, but I was too afraid to swallow the pills I had collected. I decided I would run away, but I was too afraid of the dark.

That's when God must have said, "I'm going to save this girl before she really hurts herself." And He did.

My church youth group had decided to participate in a special event that was taking place in another church. But we were late getting there

> *I put fear on notice that it could not make me its slave.*

because of a snowstorm, and since many people had congregated toward the back of the room, we ended up sitting on the front row. There were four thousand kids at the place, listening to Thurlow Spurr and his group, The Spurrlows. But when he got to his message, talking so simply and clearly about John 3:16, it was as though my name was embedded in the verse—as though "For God so loved the world" meant "For God so loved . . . me."

This man was telling me that the God of history had come down and died on the cross for a skinny, little black girl in Philadelphia, and that all I had to do to know this loving God was to reach out and receive Him.

I had never known a father who loved me and wanted me to be near him. My mother wasn't the kind who expressed love easily to her children. I never remember her hugging me. I never remember her telling me she loved me. But that snowy day in March 1965, I met the One who had said to His Father, "Whoever comes to me I will never cast out" (John 6:37). I became a new person that day by the power and grace of God.

And standing in my house those many years later, resolving to God that I would not embarrass Him, my husband, or myself, I put fear on notice that it could not make me its slave, forcing me to do whatever it demanded of me, trying to make me forget all that my Father had done for me in Christ Jesus.

## It's Resolutionary

Here's what God showed me to do if I wanted to make good on my resolution. And if you are facing now the same kind of fear trauma I was dealing with in that awful autumn not so very long ago—or worse—I urge you to take this surrendered approach to victory.

Instead of listening to myself, I needed to start talking to myself.

I started going into the bathroom, looking right into that mirror, and saying, "I know that God loves me. Yes, I'm afraid right now—afraid to move forward, afraid to be honest, afraid of what's coming. I don't know what's going to happen. But I do know that if He can part the Red Sea and raise a dead Jesus, He can surely take hold of the problems I have—even this incredibly heavy sense of fear, emptiness, and loneliness—and make me walk in such a way that I don't embarrass or disgrace Him."

And with His ever-present help, that's what I did. I had resolved it, and He enabled me to live it. And you can too, putting into practice the biblical imperatives found in James 4:7–10:

> *Submit yourselves therefore to God. Resist the devil, and he will flee from you. Draw near to God, and he will draw near to you. Cleanse your hands, you sinners, and purify your hearts, you double-minded. Be wretched and mourn and weep. Let your laughter be turned to mourning and your joy to gloom. Humble yourselves before the Lord, and he will exalt you.*

**1) *Submit to God.*** I finally had to wave the flag and say, "Lord, I surrender. I submit to You. I know I'm not smart enough to pull this off." Bending the knee must be our mind-set and heart attitude if we want to conquer fear in our lives.

I urge you to put everything on the table and surrender it to the Lord. He understands. And He knows what to do.

**2) *Resist the devil*** . . . and he will "flee." It doesn't say he *might* flee, *could* flee, is going to *think about* fleeing. God assures us the Devil *will* flee.

So take your stand against the Enemy in the holy, powerful name of the resurrected Lord, refusing to be his victim. You are a victor in Christ! Be ready to take up your position. Prepare for ongoing battle by strapping on the armor of God. Stop letting worry win out; stop giving in to griping and whining and complaining. Arm yourself for war. And above all, don't be afraid. The Lord is with you.

**3) *Draw near to God.*** You can be sure of His nearness, no matter how hard your fears are pressing down upon you. But drawing near takes work and faith. I can assure you that I was still having my quiet times in the midst of my emotional meltdown, still trying to pray and stay in the Word. But it was easy to think my prayers were going nowhere, that the words of Scripture I was reading were empty and meaningless.

Resist the temptation to let those pity parties drown out what God is trying to say, making you doubt the reliability of His Word and the certainty of His presence. Don't believe those fear buddies when they tell you that you're not worth anything, that you're not a mother just because your children are grown, that you're worthless because your husband walked out on you. Draw near to God in those quiet moments, asking Him to bring others around you who can pray with you. He is there. He is here. Draw near.

**4) *Cleanse your hands.*** The Devil loves to pile on, adding to the trouble he's already causing you. That's why he entices you to give in to sins that can do nothing but magnify fear by making you feel unacceptable to God, unworthy of His love and grace because of what you've done. Repent of your sin and receive the full pardon His salvation promises, freedom from the law and from all condemnation.

**5) *Purify your heart.*** I was a bitter, angry woman for many years, especially toward my mom. As I mentioned before, life with my mother wasn't easy. I understand now that she couldn't give what she didn't have, but for a long time I was too bitter toward her to forgive her all that she had cost me, all that she had done . . . and not done. Even after I was married and out from under her influence, my bitterness toward her continued to permeate me from within.

Crawford and I had moved from Pennsylvania to Texas to involve ourselves in church planting. And in the midst of the work we were doing, the slightest little thing could stir up within me reminders of all the trash I had been forced to endure as a child because of a mother who struggled with life's disappointments herself. All the while, I would often wonder why I was having to struggle so hard to grasp God's love for me, why I was having such a difficult time making good on my commitment to Him.

But deep down, I knew why I wasn't experiencing the presence of God in my life. I was harboring bitterness and anger against my mom.

One day I sat down and wrote her a letter to tell her that I loved her. This was huge for me. It enabled me to release a lot of the pent-up resentment I had been storing away and adding to over the years. And even though she never responded to it, never hugged me or thanked me—though I saw it opened on her dresser and knew that she had read it—I was able to live with that. My heart was pure. My bitterness was released. I was through condemning her for what she had done.

First John 1:9 says that cleansing our hands and purifying our hearts means confessing our sin, specifically telling God about it, as I did: "God, I am angry and bitter toward my mom when I think about how she raised me. It was bad for a ten-year-old girl to have to raise her own brothers. It was wrong for me to be strapped down with adult responsibilities at such a young age. But I forgive her. And I confess my own sin in remaining bitter and angry toward her through all these years."

> *As I was going through my emotional meltdown, I had so much pride that I couldn't even tell my best friends what was happening.*

There is freedom in honest confession. It's as though someone has opened a prison door and let you walk out into the sunshine after years of being locked away and restricted in darkness. Fear will always keep its teeth clamped down on us until we truly ask God to "create in me a clean heart . . . and renew a right spirit within me" (Psalm 51:10). Our hearts, motives, and thoughts need to be purified if we want to be set free from fear and avoid bringing shame on ourselves or our Lord.

**6)** *Humble yourself.* As I was going through my emotional meltdown, I had so much pride that I couldn't even tell my best friends what was happening. I'm part of a group of women—about fourteen of us—

who for nearly thirty years have been getting together to help each other through life. We call ourselves "The Stones," based on the memorial stones that the children of Israel left in the Jordan River after the Lord parted the waters and allowed them to pass over into the Promised Land. Our desire over the years has been to leave behind the footprints of God's goodness and faithfulness for our children—especially our daughters—that they might never doubt the love and power of the Lord. We've been through potty training with each other, baby showers, weddings, graduations, a few divorces (sadly), deep troubles with some of our children, but we've walked through it all together. Now we're all grandmothers together.

Every year in November, the Stones get away for an annual retreat. We laugh, we catch up, we share our stories, we pray for each other. And even though we're open about everything and available to talk about whatever needs discussing, I could not bring myself to confide in them how deeply fear was holding on to me. Pride caused me to think that my girlfriends would think less of me if they knew what I was capable of feeling and succumbing to. I did go to our November getaway, but I kept all of this bottled up and tightly contained.

Saying "everything's fine" is not the way we're delivered from the fear that can roll over us, not when it's burying us in anxiety and worry, paralyzing us from going to others or even to God.

## It's Not All Good, but It Is All God

October 19 wasn't the end of the road for me after my emotional breakdown; it was just the beginning. November is my birthday month, so as the calendar began to roll that direction, I forced myself to go through with my annual round of doctor visits, fulfilling my usual appointments with the OB-GYN, my general practitioner (GP)—and all their little test-takers.

The OB doctor gave me a good report but sent me for a mammogram, which had always been nothing more than a temporary ordeal to endure. But this time—wouldn't you know it?—I got a call back. Something had shown up on my mammogram, and I was told to come in for a recheck.

But no time slots were available for three weeks. What do you think my fear buddies had to say about that?

The GP visit didn't go much better. I was doing okay for the most part, the doctor said, except I needed to lose weight, lower my cholesterol, and watch my blood pressure. So there I was, turning into a mall walker about ten years before I was expecting to join their ranks, hoofing it around the storefronts, crying, and saying, "God, what's happening here? I've had an emotional breakdown in October, and now a physical breakdown in November. Am I going to make it through this year?"

The Lord definitely had my attention.

Maybe you've been there too. Crises usually aren't served up one course at a time, allowing you to focus all your energies on attacking this one thing. Mine tend to spread out like a full buffet line, one after another, sometimes bunched all together.

It was enough to put me back in front of that mirror, where I could give myself a good talking-to again. "You know what, Karen? You're a wimp. You've been doing a lot of whining and complaining because of everything you're going through. Maybe it's time you quit standing up in front of these conferences, trying to tell everybody how you've got it all together in Jesus when your life is actually falling apart. Maybe it's time you pulled down this wall of pride and got humble before the Lord."

So that's what I did. I said, "God, I surrender. I don't know what to do. But I know that *You* know. So I humble myself before You. Do what You will with me."

That is exactly where He wanted me. I needed to fall down humbly before the Lord.

I don't know what your issue may be. It could be an ongoing battle with your husband. It could be a problem with one of your children. It could be anything. But by submitting and drawing near to God, resisting the Devil, cleansing your hands, purifying your heart, and humbling yourself, you will put yourself right where He wants you to be. And then there's hope.

There's nothing our God can't do.

When Joshua was tasked with taking over as leader of the Hebrew people after the death of Moses, his fears must have shot off the charts. It had always been Moses, reliable Moses, larger-than-life Moses. Joshua could hardly have felt capable of filling the shoes of one who had brought them so far and led them so well. But God met Joshua right out of the starting gate, reminding him repeatedly to "be strong and courageous . . . be strong and *very* courageous . . . do not be frightened, and do not be dismayed, for the Lord your God is with you wherever you go" (Joshua 1:6–7, 9).

Of all the things we must resolve to do when life is at its hardest and our fears are at their worst, the first is to resolve to surrender. Stop listening to yourself, and start talking to yourself. Let God be God, and fear will eventually bow down to its Conqueror.

# God's
# jewels

## JONI EARECKSON TADA

Not far from the Maryland farm where I grew up was a stone quarry called Sylvan Dell. When I was little, my sisters and I would ride our horses by there all the time. Daddy told us to be careful to stay on the trail when we were out that way because the ground, not twenty feet from the path, dropped into this sheer cliff that plunged to the bottom of the quarry.

The quarry was a noisy, busy place. A lot of hammering, a lot of dust, a lot of hard work and sweat. There were steam shovels everywhere and big trucks moving rocks around, providing flagstone for the new housing developments that were cropping up out of the Maryland farmland.

But not only did this quarry produce flagstone; it also yielded beautiful quartz crystal. When we would ride our horses along the nearby trails, little bits of sparkling quartz would line either side of the bridle path, all shiny and glittering in the sun. We would hop down to touch them and to see them up close, pretending that we were walking on diamonds, as though someone had opened a treasure chest and scattered precious jewels everywhere.

It made me think of the old Sunday school song we used to sing:

When He cometh, when He cometh
To make up His jewels,
All His jewels, precious jewels,
His loved and His own.

Like the stars of the morning,
His bright crown adorning,
They shall shine in their beauty,
Bright gems for His crown.[1]

The Bible talks about this very thing—this glittering, dazzling, glorious sight. Malachi 3 describes how the Lord has a book in which all the names of those who love Him are written down. And He calls these people His jewels, His treasures (vv. 16–17).

But how do we become jewels that glitter for the King? How do we become treasures that really shine?

## Scrubbing Troubles

You and I are probably not into "bling" as much as some women we know, but I certainly like to see my wedding ring really sparkle. When it's gotten somewhat dull and lost some of its glimmer, when I'm wanting it to get its dazzle back, I'll ask my "get-up" girl in the morning to scrub my ring with a toothbrush.

A real stone like that can take a good scrubbing, you know. Authentic jewelry is not as delicate as we think. That's why God can say, as He did in Zechariah 13:9, "I will . . . refine them as one refines silver, and test them as gold is tested." I long to be a jewel that does not cringe when God chooses to give my soul a hard scrubbing every now and then.

Now I'm not glorifying the suffering it takes to polish my faith. But I *am* glorifying the God whose image is reflected on the surface of any smile that has been forced to fight through pain and problems to get there. If you want to shine with His glory, it will be on His terms. It will be the glow of *His* godliness in your life—*His* patience, *His* perseverance, gleaming through your eyes.

This conviction that the Father is worth trusting and obeying no matter how painful the trial—this calling to be refined like silver and tested like gold—is something my forty years in

> *Sometimes I think, "Lord, I'm a quadriplegic. Don't be too hard on me here."*

a wheelchair have taught me. Like a chunk of rock hewn from the quarry, my soul is not as delicate as I would like to believe.

Sometimes I think, "Lord, I'm a quadriplegic. Don't be too hard on me here." But, no, my soul can stand a good scrubbing . . . because I've not yet arrived. So He allows pain. He allows me to struggle with things like confinement and claustrophobia. He does it to all of us. He may be allowing you to deal with a pinched nerve that won't heal, a pregnancy test that (again) comes back negative, multiple sclerosis that doesn't halt, a teenager who keeps sneaking drugs, a parent's Alzheimer's that doesn't regress, a marriage that never gets any better, a job promotion that never comes, an engagement ring that never arrives.

I know that's how He's dealt with me. My paralysis has never gone away. And it has been a hard scouring, let me tell you. The issues you're dealing with today may be no less painful to the touch.

Job was right when he said, "Man is born to trouble as the sparks fly upward" (Job 5:7). Jesus was right when He said, "In the world you will have tribulation" (John 16:33). Trouble is the textbook that teaches us who we really are. Trouble is what squeezes the lemon inside of us, revealing the stuff of which we are made. And it's not always pretty.

I'll confess—when I'm in pain, I sometimes implode. I collapse in defeat. And if I let it simmer, not going to God's Word, not turning to Him in prayer, I become selfish, impatient, irritated, mean-spirited. I get this peevish, sour attitude about me. I'm just being honest here.

Maybe when trouble comes your way, you've got a smile for everybody at the supermarket and the clothing store, but you leave it right there at the checkout counter when you head home. After putting on your public face, you draw into yourself and drown in hopeless despair and pity.

Or maybe when trouble comes, you develop a lazy approach to God's Word. I know this happens to me. Unbelief drags down your prayers, you begin snapping at the kids and your husband, you stew throughout a worship service, preoccupied with the week ahead and its problems.

> *God cares most, not about making us comfortable, but about teaching us to grow up spiritually.*

Perhaps you become tired, indifferent, stale, sour, itching to get things turned around and going your way. That's when God often gets out the toothbrush, knowing there's still more dirt, scum, and impurities that need to be scoured away.

Refined like gold. Tested like silver.

Here it is, plain and simple: The core of God's plan is to rescue us from our sin. Yes, He did that back at the cross, but this whole sanctification thing takes awhile. And the resistance we put up only prolongs the process. Yet the Father in heaven—knowing what we need much better than we do—is bent on conforming us to the image of His Son.

This means getting rid of sin. Yes, to be made like Jesus is to become kind and gentle and thoughtful and compassionate, but first—if you really want to be like Christ—you must learn to hate sin. To be like Jesus is to be made sinless.

Listen, God is concerned about our poverty and pain. He cares about your broken heart and my broken neck. But these things are not His ultimate focus. They are merely symptoms of the real problem, vines growing from the root. God cares most, not about making us comfortable, but about teaching us to hate our transgression and to grow up spiritually—to love Him. That's the purpose behind the toothbrush—the refining, the chipping, the polishing.

When I'm in pain, for instance—I mean really hurting—when I've taken all the Vicodin I can stomach to dull the agony, when I've positioned and repositioned myself in this wheelchair more times than I can count, my husband and my girlfriends know I'm going to drive them crazy. So do I. And that's when I see it. When I'm hurting, I am able to see sin for the poison it is. God squeezes with His sovereign hand, and the lemon in me flows out, not usually in a trickle of complaints but in a steady stream of frustration. "God, this isn't right!" I protest. "Come on! I'm already a quadriplegic. Isn't that enough suffering without adding any more to it?"

Not too pretty, is it?

But my wise and sovereign God takes one form of evil—my suffering—and turns it on its head to defeat an even worse evil—my sin and self-centeredness.

And, oh, He is an expert at this. So when you and I yield to His sovereign plan, when we cling to the Man of Sorrows for dear life, when we rush to the cross where every ugly thing is put to death, we find our sin being sandblasted away, resulting in His image shining forth from our souls—tested and refined, glowing with the glory of God.

## Jewelry Repair

You may be thinking: "That's nice for you to say, Joni, but isn't this all a little heavy-handed?" I assure you, we should be grateful for God's sovereignty, even those many aspects of it that we cannot understand. For if He weren't in control, evil would come barreling at us *un*controlled. Be happy to leave this issue of God's sovereignty in the hands of a wise and good God who uses suffering to break apart our rocks of resistance, the way the skilled men used to do it with their hammers and heavy machinery at the Sylvan Dell quarry.

Suffering is a chisel in the hand of God to chip away our pride, to bring low our stiff-necked, stubborn rebellion. And the hammering is not going to end until we completely reflect that marvelous image of our precious Jesus, until we become holy the way He is holy. And there's no chance of that happening on this side of eternity, so we'd just better get used to it.

This whole lesson was brought home to me through a special pair of earrings. The first time I saw them, they were gracing the ears of my girlfriend Anne, a board member with *Joni and Friends*. We were together at a hotel registration desk after one of our board meetings, when I looked up at her and said, "Anne, what beautiful earrings you're wearing!"—to which she immediately began taking them off and placing them on my ears.

"No, no," I said, "please don't give me your earrings!" But my hands don't work, you know, which limits my ability to protest very hard. Suffice it to say, I was now the proud owner of $900 gold earrings, made precious to me not because of their price but simply because my dear friend Anne had given them to me.

Those earrings became my absolute favorite. I wore them all the time. In fact, I was wearing them at work one day, talking on the telephone— one of those gooseneck receiver types that I can use hands free just by resting my head against it—when I felt the earring slip off. It startled me a moment, but I kept on with my conversation. I knew that when I hung up, I'd find it in my lap or on the floor beside my desk. But after disengaging the call and backing up a bit, I still couldn't locate it. You know how it is—the lost item should be right there, but it's rolled out of sight, even though you can't imagine it going very far.

I began wheeling toward my office door to ask my secretary, Francie, to come help me find it, when—*clunk, clunk!*—a sickening sound crunched from underneath my chair. Immediately I knew what had happened. I had impaled this expensive gold earring with one of my wheels.

Francie got down on her knees to assess the damage, holding up the mangled mess for me to see. I was devastated. My favorite set— destroyed!—by me!

That weekend, I took both earrings to a local jeweler at the mall, set them side by side on the counter, and asked, "Sir, can you please make this mangled earring here look like the other one there?"

He rubbed his chin, analyzed the situation carefully, and said, "Well, lady, I can't make that one look like *this* one, but I can make this one look like *that* one." I couldn't believe what he was proposing! "No sir," I said, "these are really expensive earrings."

"Don't worry, sweetheart," he said, "I'm an expert at this."

So off he went, disappearing into a back room, from whence I could hear the unsettling bang-bang-banging of my one good earring being destroyed by this self-proclaimed, so-called master craftsman. I didn't know what I'd see when he returned, holding out in both hands what used to be my favorite gold earrings. No longer smooth and pristine, they now contained little crinkles, bends, and cracks that reflected the light of the jewelry shop, casting new colors and character off their hammered facets.

And amazingly, they were even more beautiful than before! They had certainly taken on a different shape, but I must say, they're better for the battering. They're unlike any piece of jewelry I own, and that makes them all the more special.

## Battered and Better

When I broke my back, it wasn't like being presented with a jigsaw puzzle I was supposed to solve really fast. Nor was it a quick jolt to get me back on spiritual track. Instead it was as though God was saying—as the jeweler said to me over the sales counter of his shop—"Sweetheart, I'm an expert. I know how to fix this." Truly, my spinal cord injury has ended up changing me forever. This paralysis has become a long, arduous process of being hammered into a different shape by the refining hand of God.

When my girlfriend Melanie was first told that the child she was carrying would have multiple disabilities, she collapsed into her husband's arms and cried, "Oh no, things are never going to be the same," to which he wisely replied, "Well, honey, maybe God doesn't *want* things to be the same."

How true. He doesn't.

One night recently, I was awakened in the wee hours by a stabbing pain—straight out of nowhere. "Oh no, God," I thought to myself. "Not now, not this! I can't reach for the pain pills. I don't want to wake my husband. What do I do?"

But in the next instant, I decided to grit my teeth and drastically obey rather than collapse into selfishness and fear and claustrophobia. I began whispering the Word of God into my anxious heart, calming my raging nerves and anxieties. Pulling from my arsenal of memorized songs and snippets of Scripture, I meditated on the appeal of Psalm 119:153—"Look on my affliction and deliver me, for I do not forget your law."

> *It's through obeying in small, yet great ways, that God miraculously changes you.*

And you know what? In the quiet of the night, my God *did* deliver me. I yielded to Him, and He changed me. I took a different tack than usual, and He gave me courage from His abundant supply. Suddenly I began to genuinely experience the peace that passes all human understanding (see Philippians 4:7), and I—like my costly earrings—became better for the battering. When I woke up the next morning, my character looked a little different. I had taken on a somewhat different shape. I had been slightly transformed from glory to glory.

Growing in the Lord works exactly this way. You don't sit passively in front of a Bible and just hope it somehow happens to you by osmosis. No, it's through obeying in small, yet great ways, that God miraculously changes you. You begin experiencing this sense of freedom—freedom from the bondage of sin and self.

Since the time I obeyed the Lord that night and whispered His Word into my troubled soul, I am more the Joni Eareckson Tada that He has purposed me to be. I'm a little more distinctive now. I'm unlike any other jewel in my Father's collection.

The simple formula for all of this is found in 1 John 2:5, where the Scripture says, "Whoever keeps his word, in him truly the love of God is perfected. By this we may know that we are in him." This is how we receive our assurance of being "in Christ"—by watching what happens when God, the Master jeweler, draws up obedience from the souls of women who otherwise would kick back, rebel, and exert independence. The fruit of the submitted heart is the proof that God is working—and working for our good.

He rules. He orders. He commands. He knows exactly how to handle that hammer, and He is committed to do good toward you. Just remember that His idea of good is to make you more like Jesus. And if our Savior learned obedience through the things He suffered (see Hebrews 5:8), should the Master expect less from you and me?

God says in Jeremiah 32:41, "I will rejoice in doing them good, and I will plant them in this land in faithfulness, with"—get this—"all my heart and all my soul." Heart and soul, God is happy to give you more than enough help from His end. Abundantly more. For if grace abounds where sin abounds, as the Bible says (see Romans 5:20), then grace also abounds where suffering abounds.

Oh, I want to be where God's grace is, don't you? I want the desire and power to do His will, flowing from His hand as He changes me evermore into the likeness of His Son. This grace of His is sufficient for my paralysis and for your pain and your problems, for your struggling marriage or singleness, for your dead-end job or deadbeat employees, because Jesus Christ is your colaborer. He has already been tempted and tried. He is with you! And it is worth it all to discover Him and the fellowship of His sufferings (see Philippians 3:10). Oh, the sweetness! Oh, the delight!

I tell you, His love is better than life, for "like the stars of the morning, His bright crown adorning, [we] will shine in His beauty, bright gems for His crown."

Truly, the Man of Sorrows becomes our Lord of joy when, as the Word says in Hebrews 12:12–13, we strengthen our feeble, "drooping hands," when we invigorate our tired, "weak knees," when we make straight, sure, obedient paths for our feet, "so that what is lame may not be put out of joint but rather be healed."

Ah, being healed.

You know, I consider myself healed. No, I'm still confined to this wheelchair, but I'm armed with the full confidence that health and wholeness, maturity and completeness, will be totally mine one day, just as it will be yours. And then—with joy—the hammer and the chisel will be put away. Just two minutes in heaven will be worth it all.

## Going and Glowing

Maybe you feel as though someone were scrubbing your soul raw today with a gigantic toothbrush. And it hurts. It's hard. You wince at the pain, even at the disappointment of having to bear it all.

I know what you mean. I share your pain. But let me remind you, you are not as delicate as you think, "for to this you have been called, because Christ also suffered for you, leaving you an example, so that you might follow in his steps" (1 Peter 2:21).

Dear sister, you're no common piece of flagstone. You're more valuable than even a shaving of quartz crystal, catching the glint of sunlight along a country farm road. You're silver. You're gold. And you're being refined by the One who knows how to make your life really sparkle.

Jesus said, "Whoever would be great among you"—whoever longs to bear the radiant glow of God's glory in her face, her demeanor, her entire being—"must be your servant, and whoever would be first among you must be your slave, even as the Son of Man came not to be served but to serve, and to give his life as a ransom for many" (Matthew 20:26–28). So if you aspire to be a jewel in the crown

> *Sure, I may be in a wheelchair, but that doesn't give me an excuse not to think of others who are more needy than I am.*

of your Lord, don't focus on the hammer as it falls on your life. Look instead at the sandblasting that's happening in the lives of others. Help them. Serve them. Look out for their interests.

This is one of the reasons why I love what we do at our ministry, the *Joni and Friends* International Disabilities Center. Sure, I may be in a wheelchair, but that doesn't give me an excuse not to think of others who are more needy than I am. God has blessed me and given me so much. And as Luke 12:48 says, "Everyone to whom much was given, of him much will be required, and from him to whom they entrusted much, they will demand the more." God is always asking more of me. Yes, I have a wheelchair, but there are eighteen million other disabled people in the world who would *love* to have a wheelchair . . . and who also need the Word of God.

So I consider it a high privilege that God asks much of me, that He allows me to travel and share the good news of Jesus, giving wheelchairs to needy, disabled people in places like Peru and Poland, China and Cuba. I am grateful for a supportive husband and family who enable me to minister alongside our teams during summer retreats where those with various handicaps—among a host of other issues in their lives—are able to get a taste of God's mercy, hope, and love. I'm not able to get to every event because of limitations I'm forced to endure—by the hammer and chisel when it operates—but I am there by way of heart and soul, by interceding prayer for those who need God for so much.

I don't want to overplay this card, but as respectfully as I know how to say it—if God expects me, a quadriplegic, to be actively engaged in my own sanctification, what does He expect of you?

If you want to increase your capacity for joy, if you want to increase your service and worship in heaven, if you want to enlarge your personal estate, don't focus on the chisel in your own life. Focus on others who need to be quarried out of the dust and dirt of this world.

## Bright Gems for His Crown

During a recent visit to the Baltimore area, my husband, Ken, and I drove down the old road that still borders Sylvan Dell quarry. Some years ago, it filled up with water from an underground spring. The trucks have fallen quiet now. All the steam shovels have left.

We stopped our car on the side of the road and rolled down the windows just to listen. The woods were utterly quiet except for birds calling—something we never heard when the quarry was active and we used to go horseback riding nearby. Sitting there surrounded by the peace and serenity, feeling the quiet wrap around my childhood memories, I was reminded of 1 Kings 6, where the writer reported that when Solomon's temple was being constructed, "it was with stone prepared at the quarry, so that neither hammer nor axe nor any tool of iron was heard in the house while it was being built" (v. 7). God wanted the building of His temple to be a picture of heaven, the work being done off-site so as not to disturb the peace of His holy place.

If you are a member of Christ's family, my sister, you are a living stone being built into a holy temple, being fitted for heaven and prepared for eternity. In the meantime, this world is God's work site. Like the Sylvan Dell quarry of old, it's a noisy, dusty whirl of activity, filled with hammering and dripping sweat and hard work and chiseling and pain, mining rock out of the stone pit of Earth. God is using your various afflictions to mold you and shape you, in order that you might fit perfectly into heaven's landscape . . . where there will be no more hammer or chisel, no iron tool of any kind, nothing that bites or causes pain. In their place will be only serenity—no more suffering to mar the glorious scene.

No pain.

No sorrow.

No tears.

No death.

This is our destiny. This is the very real place God has prepared for His people, an existence of pure perfection, created in glory by the grace of the ever-living One. This is our hope and joy and peace.

Therefore, since we know that our light and momentary afflictions "are not worth comparing with the glory that is to be revealed to us" (Romans 8:18), we must not waste our sufferings. We are believers—saved by grace through faith in the Lord Jesus—joining with Him in getting rid of our sin and serving others. We are no mere pebbles, inconsequential and without purpose. We are silver. We are gold. And we are being prepared for Kingdom greatness.

Zechariah 9:16 says, "On that day the Lord their God will save them, as the flock of his people; for like the jewels of a crown they shall shine on his land." I love the way God puts that. You'd do well to read it over again to yourself. But as if that weren't enough, Matthew 13:43 sort of tops it all, when Jesus says, "The righteous will shine like the sun in the kingdom of their Father." One day we will sparkle in His land. One day we will shine like the sun. Oh glory!

The reasons God had for allowing my accident, as serious and significant as it has turned out to be, are not the main point of my life. What ultimately matters is that "whoever has suffered in the flesh has ceased from sin" (1 Peter 4:1). My suffering is helping to put behind me the self-focused Joni who wants everything her way on her own terms, maturing instead into the Joni that the Lord my God has destined me to be, honed and polished by many years of quadriplegia.

The bridle path along the edge of Sylvan Dell can hardly be located now through all the weeds and thorns and overgrowth and ivy. But not so with the quarry of God. Our God is as active as ever, mining out more living stones by the barrelful, day after day. Don't you want to be a living stone in the hand of the Master jeweler?

You already experience trouble in this world. Right? Both believers and unbelievers deal with ample doses of pain, discouragement, and disappointment. Why not make certain that these ordeals you must face are fraught with meaning and purpose? Why not cooperate with what God is doing in your life—preparing you through difficulty and hardship for His beauty to come shining through?

So agree with God about your sin. Hate it. Abhor it. Want nothing more to do with it. Resolve that it will not steal any more of your joy and contentment, and walk away from its draining after-effects and its wicked aftertaste.

Neither must you waste your life on dry religion, choking on the thick airs of hypocrisy and empty form, when Jesus Christ has the words of life, like fountains of refreshing water for your thirsty soul. He is the resurrection and the life. He is the *Prince* of life. He is the way, the *truth,* and the life. And one day He will give to you and me a *crown* of life, as He will to all who have put their trust in Him.

If you would but turn from your wicked ways and live, yielding to

Christ and embracing Him as your Lord and Savior, He'll make sure that the trouble you face is worth it . . . because He knows how to handle the chisel. And He's got a crown in mind for you.

Would you join me in bearing a bit longer—just "a little while," as the Bible says (1 Peter 5:10)? That's all it is, really. Just "a little while." The noise and the hammering and the hurt and the disappointment won't go on forever, I promise you. But even though we must feel their wounds of pain for a short time, they are actually wounds of love from our heavenly Father who is making us more like His Son each time we submit with gratitude, obedience, and gutsy determination to His high, ultimate calling on our lives.

Yield to the chisel. Serve and help others while you wait. You are being fashioned into a jewel for the crown of your King.

You are silver. You are gold.

You are His.

And by His strength, you will make it.

# PART FOUR

# reclaiming
# true womanhood

*Every woman, whether rich or poor, married or single,
has a circle of influence, within which, according to her character,
she is exerting a certain amount of power for good or harm.*

*Every woman, by her virtue or her vice:
by her folly or her wisdom; by her levity or her dignity,
is adding something to our national elevation or degradation. . . .*

*A community is not likely to be overthrown where woman fulfills her mission;
for by the power of her noble heart over the hearts of others,
she will raise it from its ruins
and restore it again to prosperity and joy.*[1]

—JOHN ANGELL JAMES (1785–1859)

# leaving a lasting legacy through
# **prayer**

### FERN NICHOLS

My mom and dad passed away some time ago. They were gracious and generous even in death, leaving their four children a financial inheritance that has proven helpful to each of us over the years. But more valuable than money, investments, properties, or even family heirlooms handed down from one generation to the next is a legacy of godly faith received from those who have gone before us.

And prayer is one of the most priceless parts of that legacy.

When my mom was in her final days, I told her that the one treasure of hers I most wanted to keep was her Bible. I remember her carrying it to church, making notes in the margins, reading to us from its pages as children. Perhaps what made it even more precious was that she had not come to faith in Christ until adulthood, yet she had fully and immediately devoted herself to the Lord, and He had truly brought His Word alive in her.

No, she wasn't raised in a Christian home. But I would have a hard time believing that someone hadn't been praying for her along the way— throughout her childhood, as a teenager, as a young wife and mother— asking God to draw her to Christ. One reason I believe this is because, before she ever received Jesus as her Lord and Savior, my mother used to listen to Christian radio at home. When she got up in the morning and started working in the kitchen, she would flip on a radio that sat on the counter, tuned to the Christian station. She loved it. It was just comforting and encouraging to her.

One memorable day, the message of God's love she had heard so often in the background cut a shaft of light into her heart. And God, in answer to the petitions of those who either prayed for her by name or prayed for her in general, applied His grace to my mother's life. What a glorious moment! I thank God for it frequently.

Something else God knew was that when He saved my mother for Himself, she wasn't going to view this as a slow, gradual process she could tiptoe into. Not my mom! When she trusted Christ, she jumped in with both feet. It was a 180-degree turnaround.

There was a church within a mile of our home. She didn't really know whether it was a Bible-believing church, but she went anyway. She wanted to follow Jesus, and she wanted to grow in Him. So every week she got us four kids up and dressed and ready for church—Sunday morning, Sunday night, even Wednesday night.

In fact, I can still recall some of those Wednesday night prayer meetings, as far back as when I was four or five years old. I remember sitting quietly between my mom and Mrs. Pomeroy, a lovely lady who often shared a pew with our family, just noticing the sweet expression on this dear woman's face, listening to her tender voice as she prayed. Even as a young girl, I remember thinking, "There's something sweet going on here."

It was the Spirit of God, wooing my heart through the beauty of His people, through the power of united prayer, through the love of a mother who faithfully lifted her children up to the throne of grace.

Little did she know that her daughter was taking this in at such a deep, personal level, enough that I would eventually become the founder and president of an international prayer ministry! But that's what a legacy of prayer has the potential to do. That's why being a woman of prayer is so extremely vital, and why the time we spend before the Father is the best investment we can make, not only in our own lives, but also in the lives of our children, our husbands, our neighbors, our communities, our nation—yes, even the world!

My husband's mother says that when she dies, she wants her tombstone to read, "I told you I was sick!" We laugh at that. But seriously, what do you want your children and friends to remember about you when you've gone to be with Jesus?

I don't think I could hope for a more meaningful tribute than to be remembered as a woman who believed in the power of God through prayer. That's an investment that can never burn out, never be stolen, and will live forever in the hearts of those who follow behind us.

> *What do you want your children and friends to remember about you when you've gone to be with Jesus?*

I know your life is probably a whirlwind. I know you have a full plate of responsibilities, each of them clawing at you and demanding your attention. But even with so many things to be busy about—most of them *good* things—the absolute *best* thing you can do is to pray. What a shame it is when we struggle to pray, unable or unwilling to stop what we're doing—even for five or ten minutes—not realizing that in prayer, God actively intervenes in the areas where we're feeling the most concerned and stressed out.

I am committed to encouraging women to leave behind a legacy of prayer. You cannot give a greater gift to those you love.

## Prayers of the Saints

Rosalind Rinker, a dear saint and missionary who died in 2002 at age ninety-five, wrote in her best-selling book, *Prayer: Conversing with God*, that prayer is "a dialogue between two people who love each other."[1]

I know how hard it can be to pray, especially to get started—or started back—into prayer if it's not familiar to you or if your prayer life has become dry and lifeless over the years. But prayer is not this complex feat that requires enormous amounts of knowledge and preparation before you can participate in it. Prayer is so simple that even a child can do it, and still be heard just as clearly as the most eloquent woman who has been in relationship with Jesus for eighty or ninety years. Prayer is an equal opportunity undertaking.

> *Oh, how He desires for us to talk with Him.*

And it's powerful—simply because God *says* it's powerful. He commands us to pray: "Ask, and you will receive, that your joy may be full" (John 16:24). "Call to me and I will answer you, and will tell you great and hidden things that you have not known" (Jeremiah 33:3). We wonder why our prayer life falls short of these descriptions, why God often feels so distant, disinterested in the troubles that overwhelm us. Here's why: "You do not have, because you do not ask" (James 4:2).

Oh, how He desires for us to talk with Him.

The Lord's Prayer, Jesus' model for His followers, radically invites us to pray things like, "Your kingdom come, your will be done, on earth as it is in heaven" (Matthew 6:10). Jesus is asking us to call on His name, participating with Him in seeing His will accomplished in our place and time. He wants us to take Him up on this incredibly powerful opportunity!

But I'm convinced that one of the most wonderful things about prayer is that it enables us as women to leave a legacy for our children and grandchildren. Long after we're gone and our lives are but a memory, God will still be responding to the faithful, fervent prayers we've offered on behalf of our dear ones.

I was reading in the Word one day and came across that marvelous passage in John 17 where Jesus is praying for His disciples. I've read it many times, but you know how the Holy Spirit will just impress something on you, making a verse, phrase, or passage sparkle with new life and meaning. Jesus said of His first-century disciples, "I do not ask for these only, *but also for those who will believe in me through their word*" (v. 20).

And here we sit today, nearly two thousand years away from that prayer being spoken—living testaments that God continues responding to the appeals of His children years into the future. When Jesus prayed for "those who will believe," He was praying for you; He was praying for me.

This tells me that I can pray for future generations of my family, decades, perhaps centuries before some of them will be born. And so can you. The effect of your prayers, as God works through them in accordance with His will, will be a legacy that will far outlive your earthly lifetime.

See this on display in the throne room of the Most High in Revelation 5, where Jesus the Lamb has been deemed worthy—the *only* One worthy—to open the scroll being held in the right hand of the Father. "When he had taken the scroll, the four living creatures and the twenty-four elders fell down before the Lamb, each holding a harp, and golden bowls full of incense, which are the prayers of the saints" (v. 8). Later in Revelation 8, we see the "prayers of the saints" again, being mixed with incense in a golden censer, rising before God as a holy offering.

That's how serious and valuable your prayers are. That's how alive they are in heavenly places. That's how clearly God hears, sees, and treasures them, not leaving them bound by time and space but free to be consumed in His perfect will at a time of His pleasure and good purpose.

I've seen this happen with my own eyes.

## Future Vision

My oldest son, Ty, gave his heart to Jesus when he was just a little boy. But he had some prodigal years in high school and college. I would pray for him often, saying, "God, you know that Ty has accepted You as his Lord and Savior, and yet he's walking in ways that are not faithful to You, ways that could be destructive to his life. I pray, Lord, that You would intervene and do whatever it takes—whatever that means—to bring him back to Yourself."

I felt impressed to pray Luke 22:31–32 over my son, the way Jesus Himself had interceded for His struggling disciple, Simon Peter. "Simon,

Simon, behold Satan demanded to have you, that he might sift you like wheat, but I have prayed for you that your faith may not fail. And when you have turned again, strengthen your brothers."

I wanted God to answer this prayer right away. I wanted to see change *now!* But even when change didn't come, God kept me in persevering prayer, never giving up on what He had in mind. Year after year went by with nothing noticeable to claim as an answer to my desperate praying.

God has given us an example in nature of what persevering prayer is like. For a full four years after the seed of the Chinese bamboo tree is planted in the ground, its growth is almost undetectable. Maybe an inch. Almost nothing. But in the fifth year, this particular strain of tree begins growing by as much as three feet a day, eventually shooting eighty to ninety feet into the air. That's sort of what God was doing with my prayers for Ty. Though my tearful appeals and petitions seemed to be going unheeded, lying dormant and forgotten in the ground, our God was tending that little seed of faith, making the roots strong, doing everything that was needed for a lifetime of growth to occur. We couldn't see it at the time, but God was acting in hidden ways, performing His wonders of redemption.

> *We couldn't see it at the time, but God was acting in hidden ways, performing His wonders of redemption.*

Surely you've prayed year after year for something, never seeing any noticeable progress, any movement, any hint or suggestion that God was taking your prayer seriously at all. But "this is the confidence that we have toward him, that if we ask anything according to his will he hears us. And if we know that he hears us in whatever we ask, we know that we have the requests that we have asked of him" (1 John 5:14–15).

The incense still rises before His throne.

At one point along the way, Ty found himself in a church service, secluded in the back of the room but keenly aware that God was speaking to his heart. He felt guilty. He was unhappy. He had walked away from the Lord, and he knew it. All those prayers were coalescing in a marvelous moment of God's holy timing. "Mom," he told me later, "it was as if that pastor was speaking directly to *me*." And with tears rolling down Ty's face, God's peace intermingled with my son's repentance. And today, he's serving the Lord with his sweet wife and family, bringing glory to God and standing tall as a testimony to prayer.

We've seen this same principle at work up and down the Nichols family tree.

I had always prayed that Ty would meet a godly woman to marry. He brought a whole lot of possibilities through our door—all kinds of little cuties, most of them girls who didn't love Jesus. I prayed for them. I *continue* to pray for them, even today. But I also kept praying that God would present Ty with a special someone who would be more devoted to the Lord than to anything else. God heard that prayer and answered.

I've done the same for all of our children—for Troy, Travis, and Trisha. I've prayed that God would lead them to godly spouses. I've prayed that Christ's salvation would be extended to every single member of their families, that their children yet to be born would know and follow Jesus as their Lord and Savior, that not one child in my husband Rle Nichols's line would be lost into Satan's grasp.

And I believe the incense of those prayers continues rising up before the loving gaze of my God in heaven. I believe this is eternal stuff. I've already seen two of my grandchildren receive Christ into their hearts, and I know many more will follow in this heritage of faith.

These prayers are a time investment worth more than silver or gold or anything else on earth. I encourage you—pray, pray, and keep on praying. Don't give up. God is working even now, and He will answer in His time.

## Prayer Reinforcements

I must admit, however, what we all know to be true . . . and what Jesus warned about when He told us not to "lose heart" in our praying (Luke 18:1). We grow impatient. We become fatigued. We succumb to Satan's resistance. How easy it is to lag in faithfulness and perseverance when both time and our prayers hang heavy, seemingly suspended in midair.

One way to counteract this is by committing to stay intentional in prayer every day, even if it's only five or ten minutes—praying when you feel like it, praying when you don't, interlacing every activity of the day with prayer to the Father.

But as sweet as that relationship with the Beloved can become, as tender as your ongoing conversation with Him can feel—friend-to-friend and yet wholly reverent at the same time—I believe the most effective way to counteract our tendency toward faintheartedness is by uniting in prayer with other women.

We need to pray together.

When my two oldest sons were heading off to junior high, I said, "Lord, I need another mom to pray with. This burden I feel is so heavy. My boys are going to be facing things at school that would curl my hair if it was straight!" God was faithful to lead me to another gal who was feeling a similar need. And though we couldn't walk the halls with our children, though we couldn't hold their hands and shield their minds from every would-be intruder, we could walk beside them in prayer, anywhere they went. And my friend and I did that together.

Soon there were four or five of us gathering to support one another and intercede for our precious children. I told them, "We're not going to sit around here wasting time and drinking coffee. We're going to make the absolute most of this hour we have together." And my, how those moments were filled with the intensity of our hearts and emotions, our hunger to see God work in our family's lives.

Sometimes one of us would arrive with a need so great, we would spend a significant portion of our time lifting her up in prayer. One situation I remember was a particular mother-child relationship that had become extremely strained. The child was resisting every attempt at being cared for or treated affectionately. He could hardly stand his mother's touch, bristling and pulling away from even the slightest form of expressive love.

We prayed repeatedly over this situation, and by the end of the year, God had worked a miracle of reconciliation.

Whether it was prayers for our children to pass a certain exam, or to develop good friendships, or just to achieve success in potty training—we prayed for it all. We prayed it together.

And our faith was increased.

So I've seen firsthand the importance of united prayer. I've felt what happens when women move together into the presence of God. I've tasted the fruit of Ecclesiastes 4:

> *Two are better than one, because they have a good reward for their toil. For if they fall, one will lift up his fellow. But woe to him who is alone when he falls and has not another to lift him up! . . . A threefold cord is not quickly broken.* (vv. 9–10, 12)

Truly, God has called us to partnering in prayer. We know what happened in the book of Acts when the disciples entered together into prayer after Jesus ascended to the Father—the Spirit descended from on high, and the whole world was turned upside down!

We know what Jesus said: "If two of you agree on earth about anything they ask, it will be done for them by my Father in heaven. For where two or three are gathered in my name, there am I among them" (Matthew 18:19–20).

We know that "unity of the faith" is a key contributor to our becoming strong and mature, growing toward the "fullness of Christ" (Ephesians 4:13). "When each part is working properly" (v. 16), the whole body is built up in love, discovering the power of God in our midst.

This is God's design—the way we're supposed to work together. If I'm like the thumb, someone else is like the pointer finger, the middle finger, the ring finger, the pinkie finger. Others are like the hip, the heart, the foot, the shoulder. When the body comes together in prayer, we experience the fullness of Christ under His headship. We each do our part, and God unites us into a fully functioning church.

Don't you learn things when you hear other people pray? The disciples obviously saw something in Jesus that motivated them to ask, "Lord, teach us to pray" (Luke 11:1). Sometimes in our prayer group, another mom will be praying for her granddaughter or grandson, and I'll think to myself, "Oh, if I would've thought of that, I'd have prayed the very same way." It helps me. I write things down that other women pray, learning from the way they express their thoughts to the Father.

> *Our Father hears our wordless, groaning prayers. He hears and understands.*

Sometimes the pain is so deep, we just groan together. We don't know what to say. Words won't come. Sometimes the only thing we know to say is just the name of our sweet Lord, "Jesus, oh Jesus." But God is not like me as a grandparent, trying to understand what one of my little grandchildren is jabbering about, asking her to point to what she's wanting, needing her help to see what she needs. Our Father hears our wordless, groaning prayers. He hears and understands.

And as we pray, we grow stronger together. We become like a magnifying glass, catching the rays of the sun, the synergy of our prayers binding us together over a person, situation, or circumstance until we see a change in what we're praying for. God intervenes, and our faith is bolstered anew.

Our group was praying together for one of my high school–age sons, and—thinking of the magnifying glass—I remember praying, "Oh Lord, put the fire of Your Holy Spirit on this boy. Burn up the sin in his life until all that's left is passionate devotion for You." Our prayers are stronger when we're praying together. God delights in hearing us call out to Him in one accord.

And honestly, it's just a joy to get to know other believing women in such an intimate way, through our shared prayers for each other. To hear someone else speaking your child's name in prayer, to know that someone else cares, to clasp hands with a friend who totally understands what you're going through as a wife and mother, as a single woman or concerned daughter—it's precious.

Prayer is always available, no matter where you are. But being able to pray with others about the needs and concerns of your heart is a blessing beyond words, beyond all you've ever experienced before.

## Four Powerful Prayers

We know from James 5:16 that "the prayer of a righteous man [or woman] is powerful and effective" (NIV). Those are certainly the kind of prayers we want to offer up—powerful and effective, transforming hope into action. The Bible speaks to at least four types of praying that take our relationship with God into that category.

**1) *Prayers of praise.*** Psalm 9:10 says, in praise of God, "Those who know your name put their trust in you, for you, O Lord, have not forsaken those who seek you." We may be able to rattle off some of the attributes of God, but those who really enter into praise are those who have come to "know" Him—not just intellectually, but experientially—as the One who is strong, compassionate, faithful, almighty.

I'm teaching my grandchildren a little five-finger play that helps them remember some of the attributes of God. As they hold up each finger of their hand, I want them to be able to remind themselves that God is . . .

- *Always there.* "For he has said, 'I will never leave you nor forsake you'" (Hebrews 13:5).
- *Always answers.* "When the righteous cry for help, the Lord hears and delivers them out of all their troubles" (Psalm 34:17).
- *Always understands.* "For he knows our frame; he remembers that we are dust" (Psalm 103:14).
- *Always forgives.* "If we confess our sins, he is faithful and just to forgive us our sins and to cleanse us from all unrighteousness" (1 John 1:9).
- *Always loves.* "I have loved you with an everlasting love; therefore I have continued my faithfulness to you" (Jeremiah 31:3).

In perilous times like these, when the "foundations" feel as though they're being "destroyed" (Psalm 11:3)—when we are desperate for our prayers to be powerful and effective—the Scripture asks, "What can the righteous do?" We can remember that "the Lord is in his holy temple; the Lord's throne is in heaven; his eyes see, his eyelids test, the children of man" (Psalm 11:4). When all around us is shaking, we are told to raise our eyes, to see the Lord "high and lifted up" (Isaiah 6:1). "Therefore we will not fear though the earth gives

> *There is power in repentance, and there is power in purity.*

way, though the mountains be moved into the heart of the sea, though its waters roar and foam, though the mountains tremble at its swelling" (Psalm 46:2–3). Prayers of praise keep us from being shaken.

**2)** *Prayers of confession.* We tend to be a lot more drawn to the "powerful and effective" part of James 5:16 and to skip over the word that's intended to describe the person who's doing the praying—"righteous." But there is power in repentance, and there is power in purity.

Sin is like sediment that clogs up a drain so water can't get through. Confession is what unclogs the sin in our hearts so that Christ can live His life freely and unhindered through us, resulting in prayers that are effective, in results that are powerful.

Therefore, "let us draw near with a true heart in full assurance of faith, with our hearts sprinkled clean from an evil conscience and our bodies washed with pure water. Let us hold fast the confession of our hope without wavering" (Hebrews 10:22–23). Prayers of confession unleash the tremendous power of our trustworthy God. They become Holy Spirit–directed prayers, not self-directed prayers.

**3)** *Prayers of thanksgiving.* We are so eager to find and understand the will of God, for we know that His will is a place of power and effectiveness. Living there gives us assurance that we are within His care and keeping. Well, here is one of the things He wills: "Give thanks in all circumstances; for this is the will of God in Christ Jesus for you" (1 Thessalonians 5:18).

He deserves our thanks—"in all circumstances"—even during those times when the answers don't seem to be coming. That's when we pray, "God, apparently You're doing something that I'm not able to see just yet, and I'm thankful that You haven't forgotten me. I'm thankful to know You're working in ways my senses can't perceive."

Because it's so hard for us to stay thankful—and because it's so easy for us to forget—I suggest that you keep a prayer journal. I love going back to see prayer requests I was making weeks, months, and even years ago. Sometimes I'll come across an entry written at some date in the past, and say, "Oh Lord, You answered that prayer three months ago, and I never came back to thank You for it." There are always ample reasons to express gratitude to God, even if they hide behind the loud ones that are urging us to *complain* to God.

A thankful heart leads to a gracious and joyful spirit, while an ungrateful heart leads to depression, fear, discouragement, and self-pity—none of the things that cause us to voice prayers that are "powerful and effective." When we're thankful, we can rest in God's plan for our lives, and we can rejoice that He "causes all things to work together for good . . . to those who are called according to his purpose" (Romans 8:28 NASB). That's the hallmark of thankful praying. It changes our whole outlook and attitude.

**4) *Prayers of intercession.*** Two of the terms Scripture uses to guide our praying are the words "supplication" and "intercession." Supplications are prayers we make for ourselves and our own needs—prayers we are encouraged and invited to make. But intercession is praying for the needs of others, and it is Christ-like to pray this way.

The Word of God is a wonderful aid in intercession. God says of the Word "that goes out from my mouth; it shall not return to me empty, but it shall accomplish that which I purpose, and shall succeed in the thing for which I sent it" (Isaiah 55:11). When I was praying for my son Troy that he would follow the Lord in an intentional manner, that he would know the ways of God that are revealed in His Word, I would often pray Colossians 3:16 for him, inserting his name in the context of the verse: "Let the word of Christ dwell in Troy richly." I prayed that prayer a lot.

There was a season during Troy's early years in college when he got so excited about the Scriptures, he began memorizing verse after verse so that it would be operating in his heart, wherever he went. He even drew up this big chart on the wall with dozens and dozens of Bible verses, all written out in their own little block. I would ask, "Troy, what does Colossians 3:16 say?"—or some other reference from his bank of memorized verses—and he would quote it back, just like that. The Word of God was dwelling in him "richly." God had responded to my intercession for him.

God's Word is powerful. And effective. And praying it over our children, our husbands, our friends and family members and anyone the Lord brings to mind can turn our timid prayers into confident, faith-building prayers. Praying the Word of God makes our prayers active, alive, and oh, so personal.

One woman said to me, "I had never really prayed Scripture for my children, but putting my son's name into a verse so that it applies directly to him has opened my eyes to how powerful the Scriptures are. What a privilege it is to wrap his name inside the Word and to watch for how God will fulfill it."

I pray the Word for people all the time. I might be driving along in the car, stopped at an intersection, noticing the person to my right or my left as they wait for the light to change. Sometimes the Lord will impress me to pray a salvation Scripture for this person—a total stranger to me but well-known to Him: "Lord, I don't know if this person is a Christian or not, but if she doesn't know You, I ask that You would draw her to Yourself and save her soul, for I know that no one can come to You unless You draw them" (see John 6:44).

Unceasing prayer. Unending prayer. Undying prayer for the people in your life and the ones He brings across your path by His divine providence each day. Praise. Confession. Thanksgiving. Intercession. These are the keys to powerful, effective praying.

Use them well. And use them often.

## Ignite Your Legacy

In his classic book *Purpose in Prayer*, E. M. Bounds writes, "God shapes the world by prayer. Prayers are deathless. The lips that uttered them may be closed in death, the heart that felt them may have ceased to beat, but the prayers live before God, and God's heart is set on them and prayers outlive the lives of those who uttered them; outlive a generation, outlive an age, and outlive a world."[2]

Wow.

We pray to a God who is all-powerful. And I am asking Him for an army of praying women—in every state and nation—who will be obedient to His call and never tire until His will is done on earth as it is in heaven, until His Spirit moves in the hearts of our loved ones and the needy souls around us.

I praise God for the legacy He started in my mom and passed down to me, a legacy I have passed down to my own children, and they to theirs. If you don't have children of your own, refuse to let the Enemy keep you from believing that God can impact the generations through your consistent, compassionate prayers. Pray for a niece or nephew, a neighborhood boy or girl, a child in your church who would love to know that a caring believer is taking his or her needs to the throne on a faithful basis.

This is our legacy to the precious people who follow us. This is our gift across time and across the ages. You may not have much else to give. Or you may have much to give, monetarily speaking, and think it's somehow valuable enough on its own. But nothing is more personal and powerful—dare I even say, dangerous—in the loving, all-knowing hands of our wonderful God than the fervent prayers of the righteous.

Pray when you feel like it. Pray when you don't. Pray when you're alone. Pray when you're with others. Pray when you wake up in the morning. Pray as you're drifting off to sleep.

Just pray, dear sister. It's your legacy to leave behind.

# a call to the
# counter-revolution

## NANCY LEIGH DEMOSS

We have considered the foundations, the ultimate meaning, and the beauty of true womanhood, as created and established by God. We have seen the battle for true womanhood and the sea of change that has come about in the last half century or so, through the efforts of an initially small band of women who were determined to "have it their way."

In spite of all the promises made by the engineers of that revolution, it seems that women as a whole today are more dissatisfied, disoriented, and distressed than ever. For millions of women, *Desperate Housewives* is not just a TV show; it describes their daily experience. Many feel discouraged by and helpless to deal with their dysfunctional relationships. Few women, even among those who consider themselves to be Christians, are experiencing true freedom and fullness.

> *For millions of women,* **Desperate Housewives** *is not just a TV show; it describes their daily experience.*

But here's the good news: We have a message of hope and grace for these women—the message of Christ and His gospel! I believe God has brought you and me into the kingdom of this world, into this era—dark and troubled as it is—for such a time as this, to raise high the flag of His Kingdom and to reclaim the lives of women who have been co-opted by the Enemy.

I believe *now is the time* for us to seek God for a movement of reformation and revival among Christian women—a Word-driven, Christ-exalting, counter-cultural revolution that will take back the ground that has been given over to the world's way of thinking for so many years.

But swimming in the stream of God's grand and holy purposes means a willingness to swim upstream—against the flow of this world. What that looks like may depend somewhat on your season of life.

*Teens*—it means being willing to follow Christ and His Word when it seems that all the other girls your age are consumed with beauty and guys and self and sex and having a good time. It means setting your affection on Christ, guarding your heart, choosing the pathway of purity, becoming a truth-speaker in your generation when all the peer pressure is going in the opposite direction.

*Single women*—it means choosing the pathway of contentment, becoming willing to be married *or* single, whichever state God has for you for His glory and the sake of His Kingdom. It means using this season in your life to serve the Lord without distraction. It means the willingness to be sexually pure, into your twenties and thirties and forties and beyond. It means being a servant of the family of God. God may want to use your gifts and training in vocational Christian ministry, perhaps even taking the gospel to other parts of the world as many single women have done before us.

*Married women*—this is a call to be faithful in a world of broken promises. It means loving your husband, praying for him, building a marriage that glorifies God. It means being faithful in the good times as well as the bad, saying "yes" to your high and holy calling of being a helper to your husband, reverencing him as the Scripture exhorts, submitting to him as a picture of your submission to Christ Himself. It means giving yourself wholeheartedly to your own man, and saying no to emotional or physical intimacy with any other man. If you've been going with the flow, being drawn away with your emotions, doing what comes naturally, God is calling you to break off these wrong attachments, and to say yes to a life of faithfulness, counter-cultural as that may be.

*Mothers*—going against the flow for you means embracing the calling of being a giver and nurturer of life. Don't let the world dictate how many or how few children you should have. Let God give you a vision for the impact your children and grandchildren could make for His Kingdom throughout the generations to come. It means a willingness to do battle for the souls of your children, refusing to concede them to the clutches of the Enemy, pleading with God to capture the hearts of the next generation for His Kingdom purposes.

*Older women*—what does it mean for you to go against the flow? It means choosing not to spiritually retire. It means not settling for a life consumed by golf, bridge, meaningless activities, and preoccupation with self. There are too many younger women who need your counsel and encouragement, too many struggling sisters who could be uplifted by your love and prayers. Take one or two of them under your wing; help them learn

> *Your time has not passed you by. You are still being called "for such a time as this."*

how to live in such a way that pleases God. This doesn't require that you know everything or that you've arrived. It merely requires your willingness to find and receive your place in God's Kingdom. Your time has not passed you by. You are still being called "for such a time as this."

For many years, one of my most faithful prayer partners was an older woman I knew as "Mom Johnson." I lived with her family when I was a student at the University of Southern California back in the 70s, and we stayed in touch over the years. I watched as Mom J continued to pursue Christ and to grow in her love for Him and His Word. I watched as she aged with grace—becoming increasingly tenderhearted, wise, prayerful, loving, and others-centered. I watched her stay earnest in the battle, living an intentional, focused life. Mom Johnson finally passed away in her early nineties. At her funeral, I met a young mom in her thirties who told me, "Mrs. Johnson has been mentoring me for years." Even in the sunset days of her life, this faithful saint of God was still inviting young women into her heart and home, encouraging and discipling them for His glory.

We need more Mom Johnsons in our world and our churches today. Unemployment rates may be high, and the options available to older people may be hard to come by. But there will never be shortage of openings to be filled with older women who desire to live out the mandate of Titus chapter two.

Let me say a word to those who, like me, are among the generation of seventy-seven million baby boomers—born between 1946 and 1964— the first of whom have now hit the traditional retirement age. Between birth control, abortion, and the long-term trend toward smaller families, there will probably never again be another generation of this size. There is a huge reservoir of untapped energy and capacity in the hands of this demographic.

Our generation has an unprecedented opportunity and responsibility to invest our lives into God's Kingdom. The question is, are we willing to go against the flow, to lay down our personal convenience and dreams and take up the cross of Christ? Will we make ourselves available for His use in the kinds of numbers we represent? I believe that from those millions of boomer-era women, there could be unleashed a massive movement of true women, who could take all kinds of battlefronts for Christ. I pray that God will raise up a Kingdom Army of true women of God from among this generation.

## Giving All

You may be familiar with the life story and writings of Amy Carmichael, who in 1895 went to India as a twenty-eight-year-old single woman, staying there for the next fifty-five years without a furlough. What she discovered in India were the countless children and young women—even infants—who had been taken captive and sold into the custody of the Hindu religious fathers, raised to be temple prostitutes. Her heart broke at what she saw. Someone had to do something about this.

God had brought Amy Carmichael into His Kingdom "for such a time as this," and so, one life at a time, she and her little band of coworkers began rescuing these children from the temples in which they were held. It was dangerous, difficult work. She had to withstand religious views and cultural issues that were entrenched in centuries of tradition and superstition. She had to go against the flow.

You've certainly heard or read how salmon swim upstream to deposit the eggs that contain their young. The journey can leave them bloodied and beat up by the rocks, current, and obstacles they face along the way. But they are determined to give birth. To give life. And when their mission is accomplished, they die.

You say, "Who would want to choose that path?" But what a picture this is of the heart of Christ—the heart of Calvary—swimming upstream, fighting against the tide, being bloodied and beaten on His way to giving spiritual life even at the cost of His own physical life.

And this, my sister, is our calling as well—to pour ourselves out in fulfilling the Kingdom purposes of God in this world. Yes, it may cost us greatly to do so. But if we must expend our last ounce of energy and even lay down our lives for the sake of Christ and His Kingdom, so be it. We will be part of that band of sisters who say, "If I perish, I perish. . . . I'm going for broke."

That's what Amy Carmichael did over all those years—risking her life time and again to rescue one more little girl, one young woman at a time—working tirelessly to salvage precious lives and to expose the works of darkness that had claimed so many. Each step required going to battle against the bastions of spiritual wickedness in the world. But she marched into the fray anyway—not in her own strength, but in the strength and power of God who had sent her there. She pressed on and endured through a handful of victories, but also through numerous heartbreaking losses and apparent defeats, trusting the One whose "well done" is all that really matters.

The issues surrounding us today are certainly quite different than those she faced. But they are no less serious and pressing. Are there not women all around us who are in bondage—to guilt and fear and bitterness and anxiety? Are there not girls who are enslaved to eating disorders and sinful behaviors, harmful addictions and dark waves of depression? Just as helpless lives needed to be rescued from the temple culture of prostitution in Amy Carmichael's India, there are women in your community, church, and family who need to be rescued from the Enemy who has taken them captive.

We are called to fight the powers of darkness in the name, the power, and the Spirit of the Lord Jesus Christ, joining with God in a great rescue operation for the sake of His great Kingdom. We're commissioned to shine the light of His truth in the darkness, enabling captives to be set free for the glory of God.

## Nail the Colors to the Mast

In July 1848, the first women's rights convention in the United States was held in Seneca Falls, New York. Organizers of the event adopted a document entitled "The Declaration of Sentiments," which they asked the women to sign. This document was essentially a list of grievances against men, and the individuals who signed the document agreed to use every method at their disposal to right these wrongs. Not everyone present signed the document, but those who did went on to make history.

For decades, Western culture has been drifting from whatever biblical and spiritual moorings it may have had. We have abandoned Scripture as our ultimate authority and are now facing an all-out assault on Christian and biblical values. Nowhere is this more true than in relation to gender issues—what it means to be a man or a woman. Feminist ideology has become mainstream, and we are now experiencing the long-term effects of an intentional, orchestrated effort to undermine what the Bible teaches in relation to gender and sexuality. We have seen the unraveling of the fabric of marriage and family.

The True Woman Manifesto, first presented at the inaugural True Woman conference in Schaumburg, Illinois, on October 11, 2008, is an attempt to make a thoughtful, earnest, biblical response to this point in history and to provide a succinct statement around which women of God can unite their hearts and efforts. The agenda laid out in this manifesto is quite different from the one set forth at the Seneca Falls convention. In fact, it is a call to come and die—to ourselves, to our own plans, to our own desires—so we can manifest His resurrection Life to our world.

The preamble of the manifesto explains that this is both a "personal and corporation declaration." It is an individual statement of mission and desire, but it also calls for joint participation and commitment. The speakers, sponsors, and leadership team for True Woman '08 joined their voices in affirming this document and calling others to do the same.

We urge you to read the True Woman Manifesto carefully and prayerfully. We pray that it will resonate in your heart and that you will link hearts and hands with thousands of other women in affirming and living out its message and sharing it with others.

The manifesto begins with a series of statements that affirm what the Bible teaches about the sovereignty of God and His created design and purposes for our lives as Christian women. It concludes with a series of responses—opportunities to say "Yes, Lord" to what God's Word calls true women to be and to do.

The context for this challenge is captured in a phrase taken from the historical vocabulary of naval battles. When navies were engaged in combat and one of the sides had reached a point of surrender, the common practice was to lower the flag ("the colors") that identified the ship. Lowering the flag was equivalent to conceding defeat.

But sometimes the ship's captain would declare that he had no intention of surrendering. In order to formalize this commitment in a visible way, the command would be given to *"nail the colors to the mast."* To keep the flag from ever being lowered in surrender, it was to be hammered into the ship's very structure, impossible to be removed. The battle would be fought and won, or all on board would die in the attempt.

The term, "nail the colors to the mast," has come to mean, "to make a firm declaration of what you believe." The implication is that the declaration may not be popular and that those who make it may be criticized. But they believe in the cause and are willing to commit themselves to it, regardless of the cost.

In affirming the True Woman Manifesto, the women whose voices you have heard in this book have expressed our determination to "nail the colors to the mast." We have been joined by thousands of other women in scores of countries around the world. And we want to invite you to be in that number.

We recognize that this declaration will never be understood or embraced by the mainstream culture; it will likely even meet with resistance among some in the church today who have been influenced by the world's way of thinking.

By "nailing the colors to the mast," we're declaring our loyalty to the Word of God; we're affirming our wholehearted commitment as women to live for His glory and to fulfill His calling for our lives . . . no turning back.

C. T. Studd was a British missionary in the late 1800s and early 1900s. He used this word picture to urge believers to commit themselves unreservedly to the call of Christ, no matter how difficult the work might be or what obstacles might be encountered:

> Nail the colors to the mast! That is the right thing to do, and therefore, that is what we must do, and do it now. What colors? The colors of Christ, the work He has given us to do. . . . *Christ wants not nibblers of the possible, but grabbers of the impossible,* by faith in the omnipotence, fidelity and wisdom of the Almighty Saviour. . . .

Is there a wall in our path? By our God, we will leap over it! Are there lions and scorpions in our way? We will trample them under our feet! Does a mountain bar our progress? Saying "be thou cast into the sea," we will march on. Soldiers of Jesus, never surrender! Nail the colors to the mast![1]

That is the heart of the voices you have heard in this book. Our prayer is that you will join us in nailing the colors to the mast, and that God will ignite a movement of women who are sold out to seeing His Kingdom advanced on this earth.

## Yes!

A number of years ago, as we were considering launching the radio ministry of *Revive Our Hearts*, I asked our ministry's Board of Directors and Advisory Council to join me in praying about the decision. I remember one day sitting in on a Board discussion about this issue, when one of the older members—Dr. T. W. Hunt, in his early seventies at the time—offered a touching, confirming response.

Dr. Hunt has been a Christian leader for many years and is a true man of prayer. He had been listening quietly that day for the most part, saying little, wisely pondering the input of others.

Finally when everyone else had voiced their opinion, Dr. Hunt spoke up and said, "For a long time, I've been deeply burdened about the increased, widespread corruption among women in our culture." He gave several examples of well-known women whose influence has been powerful and coarsening. "This has been a great heartache to me," he said, "and for years I've been praying, asking God what could make a difference, what could counter that trend.

"As I've been praying about the potential of launching *Revive Our Hearts*," he continued, "I believe that God has raised up this ministry to be a light and to make a difference, to take on the powers of darkness and corruption among women and to turn back the tide."

As I heard those words, I was certainly inspired and grateful to hear our mission clarified in such a personal way by a trusted servant of God. But at the same time, there rose up within me an almost overwhelming sense of weakness, fearfulness, and inadequacy. I did not feel equal to the task, and knew that this calling would not be without great personal cost and challenges. Perhaps you can relate to those feelings at points in your own spiritual journey.

At that critical juncture in my life, the Lord brought to mind that sacred exchange recorded in Luke 1 between Mary of Nazareth and the angel who was sent to tell her that she was to be the mother of the Messiah. In reply to Gabriel's stunning announcement, Mary said in effect, "How can this be? It's not humanly, physically possible." That's basically what I was thinking as we considered this new, expanded ministry opportunity, which would demand more of me than I had ever been tasked with before.

*How can this be?* I thought. *I don't have the gifts, the skills, the abilities!* I knew that what God was asking of me was going to require far more than I could supply. Now, years later, I feel much that way again as I consider the mission and vision of the True Woman movement. This is a big mission—bigger than any of us feels up to or qualified for.

But I love the angel's assurance to Mary—a promise I have needed and claimed many times over the years:

*The Holy Spirit will come upon you,*
*and the power of the Most High will overshadow you.* (Luke 1:35)

Who's going to win the battle? God is.
Who's going to fill you with power? God is.
"Nothing will be impossible with God" (Luke 1:37).

If I have a life verse, it would probably be Luke 1:38, the one in which Mary responds to the angel in simple faith and surrender, *"Behold, I am the servant of the Lord; let it be to me according to your word."*

Mary said, "Yes, Lord." Esther said, "Yes, Lord." Amy Carmichael said, "Yes, Lord."

What will you say? What will I say?

If you were to ask those women today, "Was it worth it? Would you do it again?" do you have any doubt what they would say? Millions of Jews spared—the line preserved through which the Messiah was to come. Hundreds and hundreds of little girls in India rescued from Satan's clutches and given physical and spiritual life. Our Savior born.

Yes, God's calling on our lives will be difficult at times. It may involve hardship and suffering and obstacles. He has not promised us an easy life—a life of comfort, convenience, and self-fulfillment. Rather, it is a calling to glorify God by laying down our lives, following in the steps of the Lord Jesus who willingly obeyed the Father and laid down His life so that we could live.

> *I'm asking God to raise up a great host of women in our day, women of courage and faith; women of compassion, humility, and wisdom.*

But when you and I see the face of Christ—and it won't be long—if we've been faithful in fulfilling His calling, we will say, "Jesus, it was worth it all for You." Would we do it again? Absolutely. In fact, I believe we will wish we had given Him more.

I'm asking God to raise up a great host of women in our day, women of courage and faith; women of compassion, humility, and wisdom. Women filled with the Spirit of Jesus—for such a time as this. Will you join me in that mission? Will you be a part of a counter-cultural revolution? Will you say, "*Yes, Lord,* I am Your servant. Take me, use me, spend me, fulfill all Your holy, eternal purposes in my life, whatever it costs"?

*Now is the time.*

*Blessed be His glorious name forever;*
*And may the whole earth be filled with His glory.* (Psalm 72:19)

# true woman
# manifesto

*Who knows whether you have come to the kingdom for such a time as this?*
(Esther 4:14 NKJV)

**We believe** that God is the sovereign Lord of the universe and the Creator of life, and that all created things exist for His pleasure and to bring Him glory.[1]

**We believe** that the creation of humanity as male and female was a purposeful and magnificent part of God's wise plan, and that men and women were designed to reflect the image of God in complementary and distinct ways.[2]

**We believe** that sin has separated every human being from God and made us incapable of reflecting His image as we were created to do. Our only hope for restoration and salvation is found in repenting of our sin and trusting in Christ who lived a sinless life, died in our place, and was raised from the dead.[3]

**We realize** that we live in a culture that does not recognize God's right to rule, does not accept Scripture as the pattern for life, and is experiencing the consequences of abandoning God's design for men and women.[4]

**We believe** that Christ is redeeming this sinful world and making all things new, and that His followers are called to share in His redemptive purposes as they seek, by God's empowerment, to transform every aspect of human life that has been marred and ruined by sin.[5]

*As Christian women, we desire to honor God by living counter-cultural lives that reflect the beauty of Christ and His gospel to our world.*

### To that end, we affirm that . . .

**Scripture** is God's authoritative means of instructing us in His ways and it reveals His holy pattern for our womanhood, our character, our priorities, and our various roles, responsibilities, and relationships.[6]

**We glorify God** and experience His blessing when we accept and joyfully embrace His created design, function, and order for our lives.[7]

**As redeemed sinners,** we cannot live out the beauty of biblical womanhood apart from the sanctifying work of the gospel and the power of the indwelling Holy Spirit.[8]

**Men and women** are both created in the image of God and are equal in value and dignity, but they have distinct roles and functions in the home and in the church.[9]

**We are called** as women to affirm and encourage men as they seek to express godly masculinity, and to honor and support God-ordained male leadership in the home and in the church.[10]

**Marriage,** as created by God, is a sacred, binding, lifelong covenant between one man and one woman.[11]

**When we respond** humbly to male leadership in our homes and churches, we demonstrate a noble submission to authority that reflects Christ's submission to God His Father.[12]

**Selfish insistence** on personal rights is contrary to the spirit of Christ who humbled Himself, took on the form of a servant, and laid down His life for us.[13]

**Human life** is precious to God and is to be valued and protected, from the point of conception until rightful death.[14]

**Children** are a blessing from God, and women are uniquely designed to be bearers and nurturers of life, whether it be their own biological or adopted children, brothers and sisters, nieces and nephews, or other children in their sphere of influence.[15]

**God's plan** for gender is wider than marriage; all women, whether married or single, are to model femininity in their various relationships, by exhibiting a distinctive modesty, responsiveness, and gentleness of spirit.[16]

**Suffering** is an inevitable reality in a fallen world; at times we will be called to suffer for doing what is good—looking to heavenly reward rather than earthly comfort—for the sake of the gospel and the advancement of Christ's Kingdom.[17]

**Mature Christian women** have a responsibility to leave a legacy of faith, by discipling younger women in the Word and ways of God and modeling for the next generation lives of fruitful femininity.[18]

BELIEVING THE ABOVE, we declare our desire and intent to be "true women" of God. We consecrate ourselves to fulfill His calling and purposes for our lives. By His grace and in humble dependence on His power, we will:

1. Seek to love the Lord our God with all our heart, soul, mind, and strength.[19]
2. Gladly yield control of our lives to Christ as Lord—we will say "Yes, Lord" to the Word and the will of God.[20]
3. Be women of the Word, seeking to grow in our knowledge of Scripture and to live in accord with sound doctrine in every area of our lives.[21]
4. Nurture our fellowship and communion with God through prayer—in praise, thanksgiving, confession, intercession, and supplication.[22]
5. Embrace and express our unique design and calling as women with humility, gratitude, faith, and joy.[23]
6. Seek to glorify God by cultivating such virtues as purity, modesty, submission, meekness, and love.[24]

7. Show proper respect to both men and women, created in the image of God, esteeming others as better than ourselves, seeking to build them up, and putting off bitterness, anger, and evil speaking.[25]

8. Be faithfully engaged in our local church, submitting ourselves to our spiritual leaders, growing in the context of the community of faith, and using the gifts He has given us to serve others, to build up the Body of Christ, and to fulfill His redemptive purposes in the world.[26]

9. Seek to establish homes that manifest the love, grace, beauty, and order of God, that provide a climate conducive to nurturing life, and that extend Christian hospitality to those outside the walls of our homes.[27]

10. Honor the sacredness, purity, and permanence of the marriage covenant—whether ours or others'.[28]

11. Receive children as a blessing from the Lord, seeking to train them to love and follow Christ and to consecrate their lives for the sake of His gospel and Kingdom.[29]

12. Live out the mandate of Titus 2—as older women, modeling godliness and training younger women to be pleasing to God in every respect; as younger women, receiving instruction with meekness and humility and aspiring to become mature women of God who in turn will train the next generation.[30]

13. Seek opportunities to share the gospel of Christ with unbelievers.[31]

14. Reflect God's heart for those who are poor, infirm, oppressed, widows, orphans, and prisoners, by reaching out to minister to their practical and spiritual needs in the name of Christ.[32]

15. Pray for a movement of revival and reformation among God's people that will result in the advancement of the Kingdom and gospel of Christ among all nations.[33]

***Supporting Scriptures:*** [1]1 Cor. 8:6; Col. 1:16; Rev. 4:11 [2]Gen. 1:26–27; 2:18; 1 Cor. 11:8 [3]Gen. 3:1–7, 15–16; Mark 1:15; 1 Cor. 15:1–4 [4]Prov. 14:12; Jer. 17:9; Rom. 3:18; 8:6–7; 2 Tim. 3:16 [5]Eph. 4:22–24; Col. 3:12–14; Titus 2:14 [6]Josh. 1:8; 2 Tim. 3:16; 2 Pet. 1:20–21; 3:15–16 [7]1 Tim. 2:9; Titus 2:3–5; 1 Pet. 3:3–6 [8]John 15:1–5; 1 Cor. 15:10; Eph. 2:8–10; Phil. 2:12–13 [9]Gen. 1:26–28; 2:18; Gal. 3:26–28; Eph. 5:22–33 [10]Gen. 2:18; Mark 9:35; 10:42–45; 1 Cor. 14:34; 1 Tim. 2:12–3:7; 1 Pet. 5:1–4 [11]Gen. 2:24; Mark 10:7–9 [12]1 Cor. 11:3; Eph. 5:22–33 [13]Luke 13:30; John 15:13; Eph. 4:32; Phil. 2:5–8 [14]Psalm 139:13–16 [15]Gen. 1:28, 9:1; Psalm 127; Titus 2:4–5 [16]1 Cor. 11:2–16; 1 Tim. 2:9–13 [17]Matt. 5:10–12; 2 Cor. 4:17; James 1:12; 1 Pet. 2:21–23; 3:14–17; 4:14 [18]Titus 2:3–5 [19]Deut. 6:4–5; Mark 12:29–30 [20]Psalm 25:4–5; Rom. 6:11–13; 16–18; Eph. 5:15–17 [21]Acts 17:11; Titus 2:1; 3–5; 7; 1 Pet. 1:15; 2 Pet. 3:17–18 [22]Psalm 5:2; Phil. 4:6; 1 Tim. 2:1–2 [23]Prov. 31:10–31; Eph. 5:22–24; Col. 3:18; 33b [24]Rom. 12:9–21; 1 Tim. 2:9–14; 1 Pet. 3:1–6 [25]Eph. 4:29–32; Phil. 2:1–4; James 3:7–10; 4:11 [26]Rom. 12:6–8; 14:19; Eph. 4:15; 29; Heb. 13:17 [27]Prov. 31:10–31; 1 Tim. 5:10; 1 John 3:17–18 [28]Matt. 5:27–28; Mark 10:5–9; 1 Cor. 6:15–20; Heb. 13:4 [29]Psalm 127:3; Prov. 4:1–23; 22:6 [30]Titus 2:3–5 [31]Matt. 28:19–20; Col. 4:3–6 [32]Matt. 25:36; Luke 10:25–37; 1 Tim. 6:17–19; James 1:27 [33]2 Chron. 7:14; Psalm 51:1–10; 85:6; 2 Pet. 3:9

## Join the Movement!

Unite with thousands of other women in affirming the heart of the True Woman Manifesto by signing it online at **www.TrueWoman.com.**

# going
# deeper

## A GUIDE FOR PERSONAL REFLECTION
## AND SMALL GROUP DISCUSSION

Most of the questions in this guide can be processed on your own; however, you'll get even more out of it if you join with others who desire to grow in their understanding of what it means to be a "true woman" of God.

### Tips for Group Leaders

#### *Format and Structure*

This resource consists of nine sessions, corresponding to the nine chapters of this book, and can be used in a variety of contexts—from small groups to Sunday school classes. A weekly schedule is recommended, but be sensitive to what would best meet the needs of your group. Encourage each member to complete the suggestions in *"Looking Ahead"* each week, including reading the chapter to be discussed in the next gathering. It would also be helpful to preview and be prepared to discuss the questions found in this guide.

Sections called *"Getting Started"* and *"Talking It Over"* are particularly designed for group interaction. If the women in your group are ready to go a little deeper, you may also want to include questions and activities from *"Making It Personal"* and *"Living It Out"* as part of your group discussion. Otherwise, encourage the women to do those on their own.

## Be Prepared

Your goal for this study should be to introduce a biblical way of thinking about womanhood and allow the women freedom to share, discuss, and discover God's pattern as presented in Scripture. Ask God for grace to lead with wisdom and kindness. Ask Him to meet with each member of the group as they process what they are learning through this study and for Him to effectively work in opening their eyes to His calling on their lives as true women.

As women discuss the struggles they face, be a wise and sensitive listener. Be patient with members who may never have been exposed to some of the concepts this study presents in relation to biblical womanhood. Allow the Holy Spirit room to work—don't jump in to defend every argument or try to answer every question. Be sure to point women to God's Word for the answers, rather than personal opinions or human ideas.

Some of the content of this book may spark disagreement. Women will be faced with statements that may challenge their thinking or their lifestyle choices on multiple levels. Don't be afraid of grappling with ideas that go against the flow of modern culture. Ask God to help you lead women to the truth with a gracious, loving spirit.

## Guidelines for Group Discussion

Establish some basic guidelines in your first meeting:

• Explain that your role is to facilitate dialogue related to the topics addressed in this book. Encourage the women to read the assigned chapters, to participate in the discussions, and to be willing to share how the Lord is at work in their own heart and life.

- Communicate the importance of confidentiality. Topics of discussion may range from infertility to marital struggles, or even gender confusion. Assure the women that all personal information will be held in confidence. (An exception would be if there are issues that require the knowledge and intervention of church or legal authorities.)

- Remind members that you are not a trained counselor and this is not to be considered a "therapy session" but is merely a format for discussion and sharing information. Women should be encouraged to seek help from their pastor or a mature, godly woman, if personal ministry is needed.

Enjoy this journey together! Encourage your sisters to answer the call to biblical womanhood and to embrace the purposes and plans of God for their lives. Feel free to direct the discussion based on the size of your group and the allotted time. Try to avoid unproductive or unnecessary rabbit trails, without micromanaging the discussion.

You may not be able to cover all the questions each week—that's okay! Depending on the amount of time you have available, you may want to select specific questions to discuss. This material may take time for some women to process, so don't feel you must rush through in order to complete every activity. The goal is not to answer every question, but for each woman to discover what it means to glorify God by fulfilling His calling as a True Woman in this season of her life!

## CHAPTER 1: The Ultimate Meaning of True Womanhood (John Piper)

### Getting Started

Be sure everyone in the group has been introduced. Share what drew you to this study and/or what you hope to get out of it.

What words or images come to mind when you think of a "true woman"?

Pray and ask God to direct your study and to give you His perspective on your design and calling as women.

Pastor Piper calls the True Woman Manifesto "a faithful, clear, true, and wise document." This document, which will be referred to throughout this study, can be found on pp. 165–69. As you open your discussion time, read the introductory paragraph of the Manifesto and the "We Believe" statements (p. 165–66).

Invite three women to read the key Scripture passages that Pastor Piper highlights in this chapter: Ephesians 1:4–6; 5:25–27; Revelation 13:8.

### Talking It Over

1. John Piper observes that, "Wimpy theology makes wimpy women . . . . Wimpy theology simply does not give a woman a God who is big enough, strong enough, wise enough, and good enough to handle the realities of life in a way that magnifies the infinite worth of Jesus Christ." He concludes that wimpy theology is "plagued by woman-centeredness and man-centeredness."

What does Pastor Piper present as an alternative to a "woman-centered" mind-set and how does this prepare women to navigate through difficulties in a manner that magnifies Christ?

2. On pp. 17–19, Pastor Piper holds up several women as examples of "the opposite of a wimpy woman." What similarities did you find in the descriptions of these women?

How do these women illustrate the essence of "true womanhood"?

3. What is God's ultimate purpose for womanhood? How are masculinity and femininity at the center of God's ultimate purpose? (The three texts which were read at the opening of your discussion will help.)

4. Share your thoughts on Pastor Piper's observation:

> *"God did not look around and find manhood and womanhood to be a helpful comparison to His Son's relation to the church. He created us as male and female precisely so that we could display the glory of His Son. Our sexuality is designed for the glory of the Son of God— especially the glory of His dying to have His admiring bride."*

5. How is marriage intended to display the relationship between Christ and the church? What implications does that have for married women?

6. According to Pastor Piper, what are some truths about Christ and His Kingdom that can "shine more clearly through singleness" than through marriage?

How can single women bring glory to God, in spite and because of the unique challenges they face?

7. How has Pastor Piper's explanation of the ultimate meaning of womanhood and your God-created mission to magnify Christ influenced your perspective on your calling as a woman?

## *Making It Personal*
1. What did you receive from this chapter that will help you fulfill your purpose as a woman?

2. Pastor Piper describes the antidote to wimpy theology as *"the granite foundation of God's sovereignty or the solid steel structure of a great God-centered purpose for all things."* Would your theology most accurately be described as "wimpy" or "God-centered"? What does your answer reveal about your view of God? How is your daily life affected by your theology?

3. Have you ever struggled to embrace your design and calling as a woman? Consider the significance and purpose in your creation as a woman and spend some time thanking the Father for His wisdom. Ask Him to reveal how, at this particular season in your life, you can live out your womanhood in ways that will glorify Him most.

### *Living It Out*

1. Pastor Piper's thesis is that *"true womanhood is a distinctive calling of God to display the glory of His Son in ways that would not be displayed if there were no womanhood."* What are some practical ways you can use your womanhood to display the beauty and heart of Christ?

2. If you've struggled with anger or bitterness (perhaps due to issues related to the fact that you are a woman) take those things to the Father. Confess to Him your need to release resentment or hurt. Ask Him for grace to forgive any who may have harmed or offended you. Ask Him to help you develop a God-centered theology and to remind you of women like Marie Durant and Joni Eareckson Tada when tempted with self-pity.

3. Many women today—particularly younger women—are not familiar with the biblical perspective on the meaning of womanhood. What are some ways you can encourage other women to embrace their calling as women? Possibilities to consider:

- Invite a few young women to your home to view John Piper's message from True Woman '08 on DVD. Be sure to leave time for discussion afterward.

- Share what you're learning with a small group at your church. Use the opportunity to inspire younger women to live out their ultimate purpose in displaying Christ.

### *Looking Ahead*

1. Read chapter two by Nancy Leigh DeMoss. Highlight significant statements and jot down any questions that come to mind.

2. Read the opening "We Believe" section of the True Woman Manifesto along with the supporting Scriptures for each.

3. Read and meditate on Romans 11:33–36. What bearing does this passage have on what it means to be a true woman?

## CHAPTER 2: From Him, through Him, to Him (Nancy Leigh DeMoss)

### *Getting Started*

Describe a place you have visited or a sight you have seen where the vastness or magnificence of God's creation reminded you of His greatness and moved you to worship Him.

Open with prayer. Thank God for the grandeur of His creation and for what He is showing you through this study. Ask Him to help you enter today's discussion with a teachable heart.

Read aloud together the first "We Believe" statement of the True Woman Manifesto:

> *We believe that God is the sovereign Lord of the universe and the Creator of life, and that all created things exist for His pleasure and to bring Him glory.*

Continue this train of thought by reading Romans 11:33–36. Use this passage as the basis for your discussion. If time permits, review last week's discussion, including Pastor Piper's statements concerning woman-centered versus God-centered theology.

### *Talking It Over*

1. People are searching for meaning and fulfillment. According to Romans 11:36, what is the sum and whole point of everything that exists? How does this knowledge help us discover what true womanhood is all about?

2. Referring to Romans 11:33–36, Nancy states: *"These words of mind-boggling praise are foundational to our understanding of who we are and who He is. . . . This passage provides a framework and context for our lives as women. It gives us a fixed reference point for our hearts."* What is that "fixed reference point"? What is the perspective this passage in Romans 11 presents and how does it provide a context for our lives?

3. *"Oh, the depth of the riches and wisdom and knowledge of God . . ."* How do these words from Romans 11:33 provide stability when a woman reaches the limits of her own resources and wisdom?

Read Deuteronomy 33:27 and give an opportunity for a few women to share examples of experiencing the "depths of His riches" while in a pit of seemingly impossible challenges.

4. Nancy quotes Pastor John Piper: *"In every situation and circumstance of your life, God is always doing a thousand different things that you cannot see and you do not know."* Provide time for women to share instances when they experienced hardship, pain, or confusion—only to realize later on that God was working out His plan in and through the difficulty.

5. How does the perspective of God's sovereignty provide protection from "out of control" emotions, rogue thoughts, bitterness, and confusion during seasons of difficulty or loss?

6. In addition to being the source and origin of our existence, God is also the sustainer of all things. Read the following verses and discuss what difference this truth makes in our lives: Colossians 1:17; Hebrews 1:3; Jude 24–25.

7. In light of what we have seen in Romans 11:33–36, what three characteristics does Nancy suggest should be true of every Christian woman?

What does it reveal about our view of God if we are *not* living God-centered lives, trusting Him, and saying, "Yes, Lord"?

### *Making It Personal*

1. Both Pastor Piper and Nancy Leigh DeMoss have presented a God-centered perspective rather than a self-centered perspective as foundational to having a life of meaning and purpose. Has God revealed to you areas where you are operating without a God-centered perspective? What consequences have you experienced as a result of operating from a self-centered perspective?

2. How do you respond to the realization that "God knows everything—and everything *about* everything"?

What is your response to the knowledge that God and His ways are beyond our capacity to understand? How should this affect your perspective when you are walking through a perplexing circumstance or difficulty? How can this knowledge deepen your level of trust in God?

### *Living It Out*

1. Ask God to put on your heart another woman who is currently struggling with difficult circumstances. Pray about ministering to her by offering practical help (perhaps watching her children one evening, helping out with a meal or grocery shopping, etc.). Look for an appropriate time to share with her what God is teaching you about His sovereignty and His eternal purposes in the midst of painful seasons of life.

2. How has this week's study affected you personally? How has it affected your view of God and His involvement in your daily life? As you continue reading the book, take time to reflect on what you're learning about His character. Pause to thank Him for instances where His sovereignty, wisdom, power, and grace, have been demonstrated in your circumstances.

### Looking Ahead

1. Chapter three by Mary Kassian will be helpful and eye opening in providing a historical and cultural overview of the feminist movement in America. Be sure to set aside enough time to read and think through that chapter before the next session.

2. Read Isaiah 45:9, 11–12 and Romans 9:20–21 and consider how these verses apply to embracing your God-created purpose as a woman.

## CHAPTER 3: You've Come a Long Way, Baby! (Mary A. Kassian)

### Getting Started

Was there any information in Mary's chapter that was new or unfamiliar to you or that you found particularly informative?

If there are women in your group who recall the feminist movement of the 1970s, ask them to share any changes, positive or negative, they have witnessed in our culture that could be linked to that movement.

Read aloud together the third "We Believe" statement in the True Woman Manifesto:

*We believe that we live in a culture that does not recognize God's right to rule, does not accept Scripture as the pattern for life, and is experiencing the consequences of abandoning God's design for men and women.*

Also, read the first two affirmation statements:

*Scripture is God's authoritative means of instructing us in His ways and it reveals His holy pattern for our womanhood, our character, our priorities, and our various roles, responsibilities, and relationships.*

*We glorify God and experience His blessing when we accept and joyfully embrace His created design, function, and order for our lives.*

Ask individuals to read the following passages that form a basis for today's discussion: Isaiah 45:9, 11–12; Romans 9:20–21; 1 Corinthians 11:8–9, 11–12.

Pray and thank God for His wisdom as seen through His creation and design of male and female; ask His Spirit to direct today's discussion.

### *Talking It Over*

1. What kinds of images and impressions do you think the phrase "biblical womanhood" conjures up in many women's minds?

Does your understanding of the biblical model for womanhood carry with it any negative baggage, fears, or concerns? Are there any aspects of being a "true woman" of God that you find it difficult to accept?

2. How is the mainstream view of marriage, sexuality, children, family responsibilities, and gender differences different today than it was fifty years ago?

3. To what did Betty Friedan attribute the "gnawing sense of unhappiness" she detected in the women she interviewed in the late 1950s? What solutions did she propose to help women find fulfillment?

What flaws do you see in Friedan's diagnosis of the problem and her prescription for dealing with it?

4. According to Mary, what is the fundamental premise of feminism (p. 59)?

What are some of the practical implications of this worldview? What effect does it have on women, their choices, their relationships, and the culture in which we live?

Do you see any evidences of this philosophy in the Christian subculture?

5. Feminism argued that "patriarchy" (a term some equate with male dominance) was the source of women's problems. What did they propose as the answer to finding real meaning and self-fulfillment?

Feminism exposed a common problem (feelings of frustration and discontentment). Why was the proposed solution inadequate?

6. What were the five main tenets of the feminist agenda of the '70s (p. 61)? How is the underlying philosophy of feminism reflected in this agenda and in feminism's approach to advancing these goals?

7. What technique, used by Mao Tse-tung's political revolutionaries, was instituted as a tool to ignite the feminist revolution? What slogan was used and how did feminism so rapidly become a "grassroots" movement?

8. What might a grassroots movement among Christian women, intended to reclaim ground lost to feminism over the past fifty years, look like today? How might such a movement be fueled and spread?

9. What is the biblical answer to the question feminism posed almost fifty years ago: "What is going to bring women happiness and fulfillment and joy in life?"

### Making It Personal

1. As you read this chapter, did you recognize any influence that feminist ideology has had on your own thinking about various issues or on how you view your identity and purpose as a woman?

2. Mary identifies the foundational premise of feminism as: "[We] need

and can trust no other authority than [our] own personal truth." Can you identify any ways you have bought into this philosophy?

Evaluate this way of thinking in light of Scripture. Ask God to renew your mind with His truth. Confess your need to submit to His Word as the supreme authority for every area of your life.

### *Living It Out*

1. The seismic changes brought about by the feminist revolution over the past fifty years have been so pervasive and encompassing that many younger women today have little concept of where we came from and how we got to where we are today. What is the value of knowing some basic historical background of the feminist movement?

Ask God to bring to mind other women who may not be aware of the history, roots, and values of the feminist movement and to provide opportunities for you to share this information.

2. Consider ways you might join with other women in your community to promote the True Woman message. Here are some ideas to get you started:

- Plan a True Woman Mini-Event using materials available through Revive Our Hearts (www.TrueWoman.com/?id=99).

- Pass on to other women resources that promote the values of biblical womanhood.

- Check out future True Woman events and conferences and organize a group from your church or community to attend.

- Start a small group Bible study or discipleship group promoting biblical womanhood.

- Pass along articles posted on the True Woman website to friends; provide copies to be distributed at your church.

• Sign the True Woman Manifesto and provide copies of the manifesto for friends, family members, others in your church, etc. Offer to discuss with them any questions about the manifesto or the True Woman movement.

## *Looking Ahead*

1. Read chapter four, "For Such a Time as This," by Nancy Leigh DeMoss.

2. Read through the book of Esther. (To get the best sense of the whole story line, read it through in one setting. Or you can read it in five days by reading just two chapters per day.) Highlight verses or record insights that stand out to you.

3. Read through the first five "We Affirm" statements of the True Woman Manifesto with the supporting Scriptures. (You may want to divide this activity over a five-day period.)

## CHAPTER 4: **For Such a Time as This (Nancy Leigh DeMoss)**

### *Getting Started*

Make a list of women (past or present) who have influenced their world—for better or worse—in a significant way. What are some qualities in these women that seem to account for their impact?

Read aloud together the following statements from the True Woman Manifesto:

> *We believe that Christ is redeeming this sinful world and making all things new, and that His followers are called to share in His redemptive purposes as they seek, by God's empowerment, to transform every aspect of human life that has been marred and ruined by sin.*

*As Christian women, we desire to honor God by living counter-cultural lives that reflect the beauty of Christ and His gospel to our world.*

Review this week's Scripture reading by asking different women to read these passages: Esther 2:15–17; 3:8–11; 4:3–16; 2 Corinthians 4:16–18.

Before moving into your discussion time, ask the Lord to open your hearts to the things that are unseen and eternal, and to give you a glimpse of how He wants to use your lives to advance His Kingdom. Ask Him for faith to respond to His calling in your life by saying, "Yes, Lord!"

### *Talking It Over*

1. Nancy challenges us to view our circumstances and our world from two perspectives: the visible and invisible—the temporal and the eternal—the kingdom of man and the Kingdom of God. She describes our lives as always consisting of "two stories going on . . . both happening at the same time." Discuss what she means and how those two perspectives, kingdoms, and stories are different.

2. How does the story of Esther illustrate these two different perspectives?

3. While her story was unfolding, Esther could not see the "big picture" of God's eternal purposes; she had no way of knowing the outcome of the drama in which she was a player. How does her story and what it reveals about God and His ways encourage you as you consider the story you are living at this time?

4. As you go about your daily routine, do you look for the "ultimate" story beneath the obvious one—the "unseen story that's always going on behind the scenes in the spiritual realm"?

What difference does it make in the way we live and respond to life circumstances, to keep that "unseen story" in mind, to remember that our lives are part of a greater, eternal story that He has written and is being played out in our world?

5. As you worked your way through the book of Esther and read the chapter by Nancy, what were some of your thoughts or impressions?

Did God bring to mind any specific situations in your life that relate to the themes presented? Do you view yourself as being providentially placed at this point in history "for such a time as this"?

6. What qualities did Esther exhibit that God used to accomplish His purposes in overcoming Haman and sparing the lives of the Jews?

7. Give an example of a time when you were facing seemingly insurmountable obstacles and your reaction to those circumstances was based on the "visible" rather than the eternal story that you could not see.

Looking back now, can you see some of God's purposes more clearly than what you were aware of at the time? If so, what were they and how has He used that difficult season to accomplish His greater plan?

8. What are some modern-day movements or evils that are opposing God and His people, where you have a burden to see His Truth triumph? Dream together about how God might want to use Christian women in our day to display His glory and fulfill His Kingdom purposes.

### *Making It Personal*

1. In what ways are you "swimming upstream" against the flow of modern culture? Is there anything in your life that is hindering you from being used as a "modern day Esther"?

Did you see any character or spiritual qualities in Esther's life that need to be cultivated in your own life? Has God used this study to make you aware of any inconsistencies or issues that need to be addressed in order for His purposes to be fulfilled through your life? If so, what will you do with what He's been showing you?

2. Do you sometimes wonder if your life serves any particular purpose in God's Kingdom? Do you believe that "you have been positioned by God in your place right now for His own Kingdom purposes"?

Consider what areas of responsibility God has given you today and ask Him to open your eyes to the influence your life can have on those around you, for His glory.

### *Living It Out*

1. Look at your "story" through the lens of God's agenda and purposes. Ask the Lord to show you some of the Kingdom purposes He may want to fulfill through this season of your life. Write down any thoughts He puts on your heart.

Here are some questions to help you get started:

- What roles has God given to me at this season (e.g., wife, mother, employee, etc.)?

- What responsibilities has He given me in this season?

- Am I faithfully (and joyfully) applying myself to those areas of responsibility?

- What gifts has He given me that can be used in advancing His Kingdom?

- What circumstances am I facing that would not be of my choosing, that I must trust God can use to fulfill His Kingdom purposes?

- Am I making myself fully available to be used by Him?

- Am I obediently serving Him and others even in "unnoticed" ways?

- Am I willing to obey His calling, no matter the cost?

- Am I living with the conscious awareness that I was divinely created "for such a time as this"?

- What disciplines need to be in place in my life to equip and prepare me for future usefulness?

- Are there any areas where He wants me to exercise faith and step out of my comfort zone, in order to serve Him and others?

### *Looking Ahead*

1. In preparation for reading chapter five by Janet Parshall, read Hannah's story in 1 Samuel 1–3.

2. What are some insights about Hannah's journey that could apply to your life?

3. Read through the next five "We Affirm" statements (beginning with *"Marriage, as created by God . . ."*) of the True Woman Manifesto with the supporting Scriptures.

## CHAPTER 5: A Woman after God's Own Heart (Janet Parshall)

### *Getting Started*

This chapter may be difficult for women struggling with issues of infertility or the loss of a child through death or estrangement. Keep this in mind as you interact; seek to be sensitive to women who may be hurting and look for opportunities to encourage and minister to them.

Read aloud together the following statements about children from the True Woman Manifesto:

*Human life is precious to God and is to be valued and protected,*
*from the point of conception until rightful death.*

*Children are a blessing from God, and women are uniquely*
*designed to be bearers and nurturers of life, whether it be their*
*own biological or adopted children, brothers and sisters, nieces and*
*nephews, or other children in their sphere of influence.*

*We will receive children as a blessing from the Lord, seeking to*
*train them to love and follow Christ and to consecrate their lives for*
*the sake of His gospel and Kingdom.*

As you open in prayer, thank the Lord for the gift of life and for the privilege He has given us as women to be "bearers and nurturers of life." Ask Him to deepen your understanding of His ways and His calling in your life, through today's discussion.

### *Talking It Over*

1. Read Judges 17:6; 21:25. What was the moral and spiritual condition of Israel during Hannah's lifetime? What similarities do you find with our situation today? How might Hannah (and her rival, Peninnah) have been affected by this type of environment?

2. What two painful realities are recorded in 1 Samuel 1:2? How does this marital relationship differ from what God established in Genesis? What type of difficulties might arise within this "blended family" model?

3. What admirable qualities do we observe about Elkanah's character in 1 Samuel 1:3–5, 8? What does his question to Hannah in verse 8 indicate about their relationship?

4. What important detail is provided in verse 5 that gives us a frame of reference for Hannah's infertility?

In chapter one, Pastor Piper drew a connection between wimpy women and wimpy theology. What did we discover is the antidote to woman-centered theology? How might we apply that viewpoint to Hannah's situation?

5. What was Hannah's reaction to her rival, Peninnah (see verses 6–7)? What might this reveal about Hannah's heart? How would you have counseled her to deal with her relationship with Peninnah?

6. Do you think Hannah's desire for a good thing (children) had moved beyond a healthy desire and perhaps become an idol in her life?

7. How was Hannah's response to the insult from Eli different than the way she had responded to Peninnah's provocation (1 Samuel 1:11, 14–15)? What had transpired in Hannah's life to enable her to respond honestly to Eli but without taking offense?

8. Read through Hannah's prayer (1 Samuel 1:9–11). Contrast her commitment to God with Rachel's statement to Jacob concerning her desire for children in Genesis 30:1. What does Hannah's prayer suggest about her theology? What changes do you see taking place in Hannah throughout this account?

9. How do you think Hannah was able to release her desire for children to God? How did this help her release Samuel once he was weaned? What can we learn from her example?

10. We have an advantage over Hannah. We can read Israel's history beyond this point and see how God used her son Samuel as an instrument to accomplish His purposes in that generation. We know that God had a plan and it involved her offspring. How can Hannah's story serve as an encouragement for women who are struggling to trust God with an unknown future?

### *Making It Personal*

1. Janet asks a penetrating question on page 93:

*Can you accept His will for your life right now, even if it's not what you want? Perhaps you desperately want to be married, but God says . . . no. Perhaps you desperately want children, but God says . . . no. Perhaps you desperately want your husband healed of sickness or some other troubling condition, but God says . . . no.*

Is there an issue where you are finding it difficult to accept God's will for your life right now? A matter in which you are struggling to trust Him?

What do you know from God's Word about His character and ways that you can cling to and tether your heart to in relation to this situation?

2. In addition to sorrow over infertility, Hannah continually faced challenges from her relationship with Peninnah. Not only was Hannah reminded daily of her condition by watching her rival with her children, but Peninnah aggravated the situation by provoking Hannah—*because* of her barrenness!

Perhaps you can relate to Hannah's pain. Is there a relationship in your life that causes you to struggle with feelings of inferiority, resentment, hurt, or anger?

How would a God-centered view help you process this situation?

### *Living It Out*
1. Talk to God about any specific situations in your life where you are finding it difficult to trust Him. Ask Him for grace to trust His sovereign plan. Confess to Him your doubts and fears and ask Him to fill you with His hope (Romans 15:13) and assurance of His loving care (Jeremiah 29:11).

List ways He has provided for your needs in the past. Record examples of His care for you. Save this list so you can review it when struggling with trust issues in the future.

2. If you are a mother, have you consciously given your children to God? How would releasing them (whether young or older) impact the way you parent and relate to them? Ask God to use your children to bring glory to Him and to fulfill His Kingdom purposes in their generation—whatever that might look like, and whatever that might mean.

3. If you've been convicted over your lack of trust in God's sovereign care, take steps to place your trust in Him. If He has revealed idols of the heart, release those things to Him. Respond to His conviction with a heart that says, "Yes, Lord."

### *Looking Ahead*

1. Refer to Psalms 23 and 27 as you read chapter six by Karen Loritts this week. This chapter will be especially helpful to women who've struggled with the issue of fear.

2. Read the last three "We Affirm" statements of the True Woman Manifesto with the supporting Scriptures.

## CHAPTER 6: Choosing Faith in Seasons of Change (Karen Loritts)

### *Getting Started*

Karen shares about a season in her life when she got caught off-guard and was emotionally blindsided by a change in her circumstances. Share briefly about a time when you were thrown by some type of change—whether expected or not.

Read aloud together this statement from the True Woman Manifesto:

> *As redeemed sinners, we cannot live out the beauty of biblical womanhood apart from the sanctifying work of the gospel and the power of the indwelling Holy Spirit.*

Have different individuals read these key Scriptures that Karen refers to: Exodus 14:14; Joshua 1:6–7, 9; Psalm 27:1–3; Isaiah 41:10; Philippians 4:6.

### *Talking It Over*

1. Karen lists ten "fear buddies" that dogged her steps at one point (pp. 110–11). In what ways can you relate to her list? How has fear affected your life?

2. Discuss the role that Scripture played in restoring Karen's heart, mind, and emotions. Why is the Word so necessary and powerful in delivering us from fear and other negative emotions?

3. Karen determined she would not allow fear to control her life and made three resolutions to the Lord (p. 112). How can a firm commitment and resolve be helpful in the process of conquering fears and "unauthorized imaginations"?

4. Karen describes taking a "surrendered approach" to victory over fear. One aspect of that approach was "talking to herself" rather than "listening to herself." What does she mean by that? Why is it so important to "take every thought captive to obey Christ" (2 Corinthians 10:5)? How can "right thinking" protect us from dangerous or out-of-control emotions?

5. Read James 4:7–10. What are the six imperatives found in this passage?

The first imperative, "submit to God," takes us back to the importance of a God-centered theology and walk. How does a God-centered theology enable you to submit to God in the midst of a meltdown? How can focusing on God's sovereignty bring courage when facing frightening obstacles? Share about a time when you have experienced this.

6. Karen shares transparently about dealing with the hurt and bitterness in her relationship with her mother. How did that bitterness affect

Karen's life as a grown woman? What insights about this process in Karen's life could be helpful to women dealing with relational hurts and wounds?

### *Making It Personal*

1. At one point, Karen was unable to confide in her closest friends the battle she was facing. Is there some struggle in your life—perhaps fear or another sin, or issues related to past pain—that you've refrained from sharing with others? What could be some of the potential consequences of keeping your personal burden a secret? What is keeping you from confiding in a mature woman who could pray for you and help you walk through this to victory? Would you be willing to humble yourself and contact a godly individual who can give biblical guidance and an encouraging perspective?

2. How is fear related to our view of God? Consider the implications of not trusting the One to whom you've entrusted your eternal soul. Go to God in prayer, confess your lack of trust, and ask Him to give you His perspective on any issues you may be struggling with. Ask Him for grace to conquer your fears.

3. Is there any bitterness or unresolved anger in your heart toward anyone who has wronged or hurt you? Would you make the choice, as Karen did, to release that bitterness and extend the grace, forgiveness, and love of God to that person?

Karen experienced release from the bondage of her anger when she wrote a letter expressing love to her mother. Ask the Lord if there is any step you need to take to experience freedom in this area of your life.

### *Living It Out*

1. Make a list of any specific fears you may be facing. Then find Scriptures to counter each of those fears. It may take you several days to

compile the Scriptures, but continue to add to this list whenever you come across verses that apply to a particular fear.

2. Choose several verses from your list to memorize and apply whenever the "fear buddies" appear on the scene!

### Looking Ahead

1. In chapter seven, Joni Eareckson Tada challenges us with her perspective on suffering, born out of nearly forty-five years as a quadriplegic. In conjunction with this chapter, refer to these passages: Zechariah 13:9; 2 Corinthians 4:7–18.

2. Read through the first five "We Will" statements of the True Woman Manifesto with the supporting Scriptures.

3. If you have a diamond ring or another piece of diamond jewelry, bring it with you to the next session, along with a small, soft toothbrush. Ask one of the women in the group to bring some jewelry cleaning solution or mild dishwashing detergent. (Avoid harsh chemicals such as laundry detergent or bath gel.)

## CHAPTER 7: God's Jewels
## (Joni Eareckson Tada)

### Getting Started

Did you bring a piece of diamond jewelry with you? Have someone pour cleaning solution or warm water with detergent in one or more bowls. Place your jewelry in a bowl and let it soak.

Read aloud together the following affirmations from the True Woman Manifesto:

> We glorify God and experience His blessing when we accept and joyfully embrace His created design, function, and order for our lives.

*Suffering is an inevitable reality in a fallen world; at times we will
be called to suffer for doing what is good—looking to heavenly
reward rather than earthly comfort—for the sake of the gospel and
the advancement of Christ's Kingdom.*

All of us have experienced varying levels of difficulty and perhaps even
endured actual periods of suffering. Joni's chapter challenges us to
embrace suffering as God's means of refining our lives so they can reflect
God's glory.

Have individuals read the following Scriptures referenced by Joni:
Zechariah 13:9; Malachi 3:16–18; Philippians 3:10; 1 Peter 2:21; 4:1;
5:10; 1 John 2:5–6.

Pray that the Lord will minister grace to each woman in areas of their life
where they may be hurting, and that He will use their trials to conform
them to the image of Christ and to prepare them as precious jewels that
shine for Him.

Now, remove your jewelry from the water. Using the toothbrush, gently
scrub the diamonds and the metal (gold, silver, platinum), removing the impurities. Rinse the diamond with warm water. Let the fresh "sparkle" remind
you of the way God uses hardships and trials to clean and polish our lives.

### *Talking It Over*

1. What insights in this chapter did you find particularly encouraging or
helpful in relation to suffering?

2. According to Joni: *"Trouble is what squeezes the lemon inside of us,
revealing the stuff of which we are made."*

Can you think of a time when God used a painful situation to open your
eyes to an area of sin you had not yet recognized? How did God work in
your life through that refining process? What counsel would you share
with a woman going through a similar circumstance?

3. Joni shared an example of applying Psalm 119:153 during the night when she was awakened by stabbing pain:

> *I decided to grit my teeth and drastically obey rather than collapse into selfishness and fear and claustrophobia. I began whispering the Word of God into my anxious heart . . . I yielded to Him, and He changed me . . . It's through obeying in small, yet great ways, that God miraculously changes you.*

How have you experienced the power of God's Word to help you make it through difficult times and to change you in the process? How have you experienced freedom as a result of obeying Him, even in seemingly small ways?

4. Joni refers to God's hammer of refining as evidence that He is "committed to do good toward you." How can periods of suffering be viewed as something "good"? Refer to one or more of these passages to guide your thinking: Jeremiah 32:41; Romans 5:20; Philippians 3:10; Hebrews 12:12; 1 Peter 2:21; 5:10.

5. Jesus said: "Everyone to whom much was given, of him much will be required, and from him to whom they entrusted much, they will demand the more" (Luke 12:48). How might this Scripture apply to those who have been entrusted with blessings? With pain?

6. Joni poses a probing question: *If God expects me, a quadriplegic, to be actively engaged in my own sanctification, what does He expect of you?* As you consider Joni's determination to let God sanctify her through her pain, what do you think the Lord may be saying to you?

7. One of the most difficult aspects of suffering is the tendency to view this period as a season that will never end. Put suffering into an "eternal perspective" by reading and discussing Matthew 13:43 and Romans 8:18.

### *Making It Personal*

1. How did this chapter influence or challenge your perspective on suffering? Can you honestly say that you desire more to be conformed to the image of Christ—to become a "treasure that shines"—than you desire a life free from pain?

2. Joni states: *If you really want to be like Christ—you must learn to hate sin. . . . God takes one form of evil—my suffering—and turns it on its head to defeat another evil—my sin and self-centeredness.*

Affliction is one tool God uses to help us develop a hatred for sin. Consider these Scriptures: Psalm 119:67, 71, 75, 92 in light of this principle. Can you think of instances when God has used suffering in your life to expose your sin? Have you developed a hatred for that sin?

3. Are you in the midst of a season of pain? Have you found yourself struggling with questions of God's goodness . . . His purpose in this . . . whether it will ever end? Why not lay your questions before Him today, and then choose to trust His commitment to "do good toward you" (Jeremiah 32:41)? Will you entrust yourself to Him as your faithful Creator in doing what is right (1 Peter 4:19)?

### *Living It Out*

1. Joni mentioned how serving in a ministry to aid the disabled and needy helps her to focus on others:

> *If you want to increase your capacity for joy, if you want to increase your service and worship in heaven, if you want to enlarge your personal estate, don't focus on the chisel in your own life. Focus on others who need to be quarried out of the dust and dirt of this world.*

Who can you serve today? Consider how you can minister to others who are in greater need than you.

## *Looking Ahead*

1. Psalm 78:1–8 lays a good foundation for Fern Nichols' chapter on leaving a lasting legacy through prayer. As you read this chapter, consider how God wants to use your life to have an impact on the next generation.

2. Read through the next five "We Will" statements (#6–10) of the True Woman Manifesto with the supporting Scriptures.

## CHAPTER 8: Leaving a Lasting Legacy through Prayer (Fern Nichols)

### *Getting Started*

Invite each woman to share about someone whose prayers have played a significant role in their spiritual journey.

Fern issues a challenge for women to "leave behind a legacy of prayer." Although this chapter highlights the responsibility of mothers to intercede for their children, this call is for all women—not just mothers.

Read aloud together the following statements from the True Woman Manifesto:

> *Mature Christian Women have a responsibility to leave a legacy of faith, by discipling younger women in the Word and ways of God and modeling for the next generation lives of fruitful femininity.*

> *We will nurture our fellowship and communion with God through prayer—in praise, thanksgiving, confession, intercession, and supplication.*

> *We will pray for a movement of revival and reformation among God's people that will result in the advancement of the Kingdom and gospel of Christ among all nations.*

Have individuals read Scripture reading: Jeremiah 33:3; John 15:7; 16:24; James 4:2; 5:16; 1 John 5:14–15. Follow the Scripture reading with a time of prayer. Thank the Lord for the privilege of communicating with Him through prayer. Ask Him to increase your heart for prayer and your vision for passing the baton of faith on to the next generation.

### Talking It Over

1. Have you been inspired by a woman who has been faithful in prayer? If so, what have you learned from her example? How has this affected your view of intercession?

2. How would you answer Fern's question: "What do you want your children and friends to remember about you when you've gone to be with Jesus?"

3. What does Fern recommend as ways to counteract the tendency toward "faintheartedness" in prayer? What things have you found helpful for your prayer life?

4. Discuss the importance and benefits of "united prayer."

5. Fern talks about prayers of praise, confession, thanksgiving, and intercession. How balanced is your prayer life in these four areas? Where do you need to grow?

6. Fern mentions using a prayer journal. Invite any women who have used this tool to share how it has been beneficial to them.

7. Why is it important to use Scripture in your prayer time? Share some ways you can do that.

8. Encourage one another by sharing a few brief testimonies of answered prayers.

9. What do you think E. M. Bounds meant by this statement?

*Prayers outlive the lives of those who uttered them, outlive a generation, outlive an age, and outlive a world.*

Can you think of an illustration of this principle in Scripture, in history, or in your own experience? If you really believed this statement, what difference might it make in your prayer life? How could this concept be an encouragement to someone who is grappling with the disappointment of (apparently) unanswered prayers?

10. Discuss various prayer strategies you've found effective.

11. Close today's session by spending some extended time in prayer. You may want to break up into pairs, triplets, or small groups. Focus your prayers on the next generation—whether your own sons, daughters, and grandchildren, or others.

### Making It Personal

1. What place does prayer hold in your list of daily priorities? Did God put anything on your heart in relation to the need for growth or change in your prayer life as you read this chapter?

2. If the spiritual legacy you leave behind for those who will outlive you and for future generations were no greater than the faithfulness, frequency, and fervency of your prayers, what would that legacy look like?

### Living It Out

1. Has this chapter challenged you to become more intentional in your praying? What are some steps you will take to develop a more effective prayer life? If you've never kept a prayer journal, consider using one for the next month.

2. If prayer is something you've struggled with, use a topical Bible or a concordance to study this topic. You may also want to read a good book on prayer, or a biography of someone like George Mueller who was known for his faith and his prayer life.

3. If you don't have a friend or group of women to pray with regularly, ask the Lord if He might want you to invite others to join you in regular times of concentrated prayer for spiritual needs within your family, community, church, or nation.

### *Looking Ahead*

1. Read chapter nine, "A Call to the Counter-Revolution" (pp. 153–63), as well as the final statements in the "We Will" section of the True Woman Manifesto (#11–15), with the supporting Scriptures.

2. Next week's session will include an invitation to sign the True Woman Manifesto. This is an opportunity to express your commitment to the principles you've been studying and your desire to be a part of a spiritual counter-cultural revolution among Christian women. By way of review and preparation, take time to read the True Woman Manifesto through in its entirety (pp. 165–69).

3. If you have time, read Mary Kassian's piece called "The Need for a Creed" (appendix A). You may also want to go to www.TrueWoman.com to read posts pertaining to specific statements in the "We Will" section of the True Woman Manifesto.

## CHAPTER 9: A Call to the Counter-Revolution (Nancy Leigh DeMoss)

### *Getting Started*

Discuss how God has used this study in your life. What particular chapters or insights have proven to be most helpful and challenging to you? What have you learned (or been reminded of) about the ways of God and His calling on our lives as Christian women? What changes have you made as a result of what He has shown you?

Consider any ways you may want to continue providing encouragement, prayer support, and friendship for one another beyond this study.

## *Talking It Over*

1. Share an example of an important document or agreement you have signed in the past (e.g., a wedding license). What was signified and implied in putting your signature on that document?

2. Chapter nine uses the illustration of a naval commander's order to "nail the colors to the mast!" Explain the meaning of that command and discuss its relevance to our lives as women desiring to be "true women" of God in our day.

3. How does the True Woman Manifesto represent "nailing the colors to the mast"?

4. What might be the impact—in our homes, our churches, our communities, around the world—if thousands of women all across this country and throughout the world began to live out the message and ideals of this manifesto?

5. Do you want to be a part of a counter-cultural, spiritual revolution among Christian women in our day? Do you desire to join other women in living out and reproducing the message presented in this book and summarized in the manifesto?

If so, we invite you to express that desire by signing the True Woman Manifesto.

By affirming this document, we aren't giving allegiance to our own ideals of womanhood, or a comfortable and self-centered agenda. We are agreeing with and giving allegiance to the model of womanhood lived for the glory of God, as outlined in Scripture.

In signing this document, you are saying, "Yes, Lord. I want to be a true woman of God. I embrace Your plan, Your design, and Your calling for my life. By the power of Your Spirit, I want my life to reflect the beauty and the wonder of Your ways, to exalt Christ, and to adorn His gospel."

### *Nailing the Colors to the Mast*

1. Pray and ask the Lord to make these next moments a sacred time as you make this personal and corporate declaration of belief, consecration, and prayerful intent.

2. Read the True Woman Manifesto. Depending on the size of your group, have one or more individuals read aloud the various statements that make up the three sections: "We Believe," "We Affirm," and "We Will."

If the fifteen statements in the third section reflect the commitment of your heart, you may wish to express your agreement by simply saying, "Yes, Lord!" at the end of each statement.

3. Sign the manifesto as a way of expressing that you affirm it in your heart. This can be done in one or more of the following ways:

• Sign online at: www.TrueWoman.com.

• Copies of the True Woman Manifesto (available through Revive Our Hearts) can be individually signed, dated, and returned to: Revive Our Hearts, P.O. Box 2000, Niles, MI, 49120. These signatures will be added to those who have signed online.

• Invite all the women in your group to sign an enlarged copy of the manifesto. (Frameable prints are available in the store at www.TrueWoman. com.) The women's ministry in your church may want to provide an opportunity for women throughout the church to sign this print and then frame the document and display it in the church building.

In signing this document, you are saying:

*I desire to be a part of a counter-cultural, spiritual revolution among Christian women. I have read and personally affirm the True Woman Manifesto, and I want to join other women in living out and reproducing its message.*

4. Discuss some ways you could share this message with other women in the days ahead. (Go to www.TrueWoman.com and search for "True Woman Sightings" to learn how other women are furthering the mission and message of the True Woman movement.)

5. Conclude your time with a season of prayer.

- Thank the Lord for the privilege of living as redeemed women and being called to serve Him "for such a time as this."

- Ask God for His grace and the power of His Spirit to live as True Women in every sphere and season of your life.

- Pray for a movement of revival and reformation in the hearts of Christian women everywhere, that will reclaim ground that has been given over to the Enemy. Ask God to ignite in thousands of other women a passion to fulfill His purpose and calling for their lives.

- Pray that as a result of this movement, Christ will be exalted and the glory and redeeming love of God will be displayed throughout the whole earth.

# join the
# mȯvement
# what's next?

## 1. Sign the True Woman Manifesto

We're asking God for 100,000 hungry-hearted women to affirm their desire to be a part of the True Woman movement by signing this manifesto at www.TrueWoman.com.

## 2. Join the Online Community of True Women

**Subscribe to the Revive Our Hearts Daily Connection.** Join teacher Nancy Leigh DeMoss and special guests for daily teaching from God's Word, designed to help women experience freedom, fullness, and freedom in Christ. (*Revive Our Hearts* is a nationally syndicated half-hour program heard Monday-Friday on approximately a thousand Christian radio outlets. Transcripts and audio are available online and via podcast.)

**Interact on the True Woman Blog** with other women about what it practically looks like for you to live as a woman of God—in all seasons of life.

**Follow the True Woman Movement on Facebook and Twitter.** Stay abreast of the latest happenings.

**Take the 30-day True Woman Makeover** and join Nancy Leigh DeMoss on a journey through Proverbs 31, 1 Timothy 2:9–10, and Titus 2:1–5. For thirty days, we'll send directly to your in-box this e-mail, filled with biblical teaching, helpful links, printable downloads, and recommended resources.

## 3. Spread the True Woman Message

**Invite others to join you in studying this book.** Ask the leaders of your church to consider offering this study through the women's ministry.

**Order DVDs or download the messages from True Woman '08** (contained in this book) to share with others.

**Host a True Woman Event** in your home or church with your friends, neighbors, and coworkers. We'll give you the tools you need with the free downloadable True Woman Event Kit. Just add your personal creative touch, and watch God transform the hearts and homes of the women in your community.

Find all this and more at www.ReviveOurHearts.com
and www.TrueWoman.com.

# the need for a
# creed

## *Reflections on Creeds, Confessions, and Manifestos*

## MARY A. KASSIAN

Everyone has a creed. Even those who say they don't believe in creeds have a creed. Their creed is: "I don't believe in creeds!" What exactly is a creed? It's simply a statement of belief. "Creed" is derived from the Latin word *credo*, "to believe." Therefore, if you have the capacity to believe in something, then you have a creed—even if it's an unspoken one.

Throughout history, individuals and groups have written down their creeds. These have variously been called Declarations, Resolutions, Statements, Statements of Belief, Mission Statements, Doctrinal Statements, Confessions (from Latin *confessus*—to acknowledge), or Manifestos (from Latin *manifestus*—clear, evident, manifest). All are essentially creeds. Written creeds have played a vital and undeniable role in history—in philosophy, politics, and culture, as well as in the church.

The United States of America was founded on a creed called The Declaration of Independence: "We hold these truths to be self-evident, that all men are created equal, that they are endowed by their Creator with certain unalienable rights, that among these are life, liberty and the pursuit of happiness . . ." The French Aristocracy was overthrown as a result of the Declaration of the Rights of Man and Citizen, a creed published during the French Revolution. Karl Marx and Friedrich Engels collaborated on a creed that changed the political landscape for generations: The Communist Manifesto. The Humanist Manifesto I, a fifteen-point creed written in 1933, was published with thirty-four signatories. It led to the 1973 Humanist Manifesto II, whose oft-quoted lines include, "No deity will save us; we must save ourselves," and "We are responsible for what we are and for what we will be." The second Humanist Manifesto was initially published with a small number of signatories, but then procured thousands more. Over the course of time, its tenets have been assimilated en masse to become the dominant worldview of our time.

Just as political and philosophical creeds have profoundly influenced the course of secular history, so have Christian creeds profoundly affected the history of the church. It's important to note that contrary to secular creeds, the creeds produced by the Christian church are statements of faith that are meant to accurately reflect and summarize what Scripture teaches. They are not regarded as additions or replacements for Scripture. Instead, these documents are carefully considered and thoughtfully worded responses to various issues, heresies, and historical situations that have challenged the church and sound doctrine over the centuries. In general, they highlight and oppose those errors that the compilers of the creed believe are most dangerous to sound doctrine at that particular time in history.

The Apostles' Creed, drawn up in the first or second century, emphasized the full humanity of Jesus. This was in response to the Gnostic movement of the time, which taught that the physical world was evil, and that Christ did not actually take on human nature. The Nicene Creed, written in the fourth century, emphatically affirmed the deity of Christ. It was directed against the Arians—a group of people in the church who were proposing that Christ was not fully God. Martin Luther's Ninety-Five Theses was a creed that countered the practice of indulgences. It became the primary catalyst for the Protestant Reformation in the 1500s. The Ninety-Five Theses preceded other creeds such as the Augsburg Confession, The Heidelberg Catechism, The Canons of the Synod of Dort, and later, the

London Baptist Confession and Westminster Confession of Faith. The Chicago Statement on Biblical Inerrancy, a creed signed by hundreds of biblical scholars and leaders in 1978, was formulated to defend against the trend toward liberal and neo-orthodox conceptions of Scripture.

History demonstrates that creeds are profoundly important. They are documents that challenge people to change, counter, or correct a current trend of thought—or at the very least, to reconsider it. Creeds clarify beliefs. Creeds set direction. Creeds create movements. Creeds are like signposts at a junction. They require travelers to choose and commit to one path or another. Ultimately, this choice determines whether the traveler and those who follow will arrive at one destination, or at a different one, miles apart from the first.

Since its unveiling in Chicago on October 11, 2008, thousands of Christian women from scores of countries have signed the True Woman Manifesto, a creed that summarizes what its signers believe the Bible teaches about what it means to be a woman created in the image of God, living for the glory of God. Given the effects of the feminist movement, the cultural assault on gender and sexuality, and the unprecedented deconstruction of marriage and the family, I believe a carefully considered and thoughtfully worded response to this historical situation is warranted. The pressure on the church to accommodate to culture's view of manhood and womanhood is enormous—the Bible's teachings on gender and sexuality have become extremely counter-cultural. Yet in and through Christ, they remain our only hope for discovering our true identity and purpose, finding healing and wholeness, and living in a manner worthy of those created in the image and for the glory of God.

The True Woman Manifesto is not meant to be a comprehensive statement of faith, nor a catalog of matters essential to salvation, nor an infallible guide to every aspect of life, nor a document that in any way adds to or replaces Scripture. As with any creed, proponents and opponents could endlessly debate the choice of wording, order, and emphases. But doing so would miss the point. The True Woman Manifesto is merely a signpost—highlighting some major points about what we believe the Bible says to women, and declaring our conviction that even if its teachings are unpopular in this day and age, the Bible provides the best (and wholly authoritative) instruction with regard to what we believe and how we live as women.

Today, many women are unwittingly living by creeds set forth by the secular woman's movement. I challenge you to consider endorsing a different creed. The True Woman Manifesto is significant. It's historic. And I invite *you* to sign your name to be part of this counter-cultural revolution.

—*This piece appeared on the True Woman blog on February 4, 2009. http://www .truewoman.com/?id=564*

# a prayer for
# **women**

## PASTOR JOHN PIPER

My earnest challenge and prayer for you is . . .

. . . That all of your life—in whatever calling—be devoted to the glory of God.

. . . That the promises of Christ be trusted so fully that peace and joy and strength fill your soul to overflowing.

. . . That this fullness of God overflows in daily acts of love so that people might see your good deeds and give glory to your Father in Heaven.

. . . That you be women of the Book, who love and study and obey the Bible in every area of its teaching; that meditation on biblical truth be the source of hope and faith; that you continue to grow in understanding through all the chapters of your life, never thinking that study and growth are only for others.

. . . That you be women of prayer, so that the Word of God will be opened to you, and so the power of faith and holiness will descend upon you; that your spiritual influence may increase at home and at church and in the world.

. . . That you be women who have a deep grasp of the sovereign grace of God which undergirds all these spiritual processes; and that you be deep thinkers about the doctrines of grace, and even deeper lovers of these things.

. . . That you be totally committed to ministry, whatever your specific calling; that you not fritter away your time on soaps or women's magazines or unimportant hobbies or shopping; that you redeem the time for Christ and his Kingdom.

. . . That, if you are single, you exploit your singleness to the full in devotion to God (the way Jesus and Paul and Mary Slessor and Amy Carmichael did) and not be paralyzed by the desire to be married.

. . . That, if you are married, you creatively and intelligently and sincerely support the leadership of your husband as deeply as obedience to Christ will allow; that you encourage him in his God-appointed role as head; that you influence him spiritually primarily through your fearless tranquility and holiness and prayer.

. . . That, if you have children, you accept responsibility with your husband (or alone if necessary) to raise up children in the discipline and instruction of the Lord—children who hope in the triumph of God— sharing with your husband the teaching and discipline they need, and giving them the special attention they crave from you, as well as that special nurturing touch and care that you alone are fitted to give.

. . . That you not assume that secular employment is a greater challenge or a better use of your life than the countless opportunities of service and witness in the home, the neighborhood, the community, the church, and the world; that you not only pose the question: career or full-time homemaker?, but that you ask just as seriously: full-time career or freedom for ministry? That you ask: Which would be greater for the Kingdom—to work for someone who tells you what to do to make his or her business prosper, or to be God's free agent dreaming your own dream about how your time and your home and your creativity could make God's business prosper? And that in all this you make your choices not on the basis of secular trends or upward lifestyle expectations, but on the basis of what will strengthen the faith of the family and advance the cause of Christ.

. . . That you step back and (with your husband, if you are married) plan the various forms of your life's ministry in chapters. Chapters are divided by various things—age, strength, singleness, marriage, employment, children at home, children in college, grandchildren, retirement, etc. No chapter has all the joys. Finite life is a series of trade-offs. Finding God's will, and living for the glory of Christ to the full in every chapter is what makes it a success, not whether it reads like somebody else's chapter or whether it has in it what only another chapter will bring.

. . . That you develop a wartime mentality and lifestyle; that you never forget that life is short, that billions of people hang in the balance of heaven and hell every day, that the love of money is spiritual suicide, that the goals of upward mobility (nicer clothes, cars, houses, vacations, food, hobbies) are a poor and dangerous substitute for the goals of living for Christ with all your might and maximizing your joy in ministry to people's needs.

. . . That in all your relationships with men (not just in marriage) you seek the guidance of the Holy Spirit in applying the biblical vision of manhood and womanhood; that you develop a style and demeanor that does justice to the unique role God has given to man to feel responsible for gracious leadership in relation to women—a leadership which involves elements of protection and provision and a pattern of initiative; that you think creatively and with cultural sensitivity (just as he must do) in shaping the style and setting the tone of your interaction with men.

. . . That you see the biblical guidelines for what is appropriate and inappropriate for men and women not as arbitrary constraints on freedom, but as wise and gracious prescriptions for how to discover the true freedom of God's ideal of complementarity; that you not measure your potential by the few roles withheld, but by the countless roles offered; that you look to the loving God of Scripture and dream about the possibilities of your service to him.

—Excerpted from *Recovering Biblical Manhood and Womanhood: A Response to Evangelical Feminism* ©1991, edited by John Piper and Wayne Grudem. Used by permission of Crossway Books, a publishing ministry of Good News Publishers, Wheaton, IL 60187, www.crossway.org.

# Acknowledgments

One of the great joys of my life is the privilege of serving alongside men and women who love Christ and who share my burden for a movement of His Spirit in the hearts of His people. My load is lightened and I am infused with courage and grace to press on in the battle, through the friendship, prayers, and partnership of these fellow-servants. Their selfless, sacrificial efforts are unseen by most and receive far less recognition or reward than deserved. But God sees and He will reward in That Day.

I am especially grateful for those whose labors have helped make this book possible, among them:

- Once again, our friends at *Moody Publishers* have demonstrated their heart to publish quality, biblically sound, Christ-exalting content that transforms lives. Their ongoing support and their partnership with our ministry are producing "much fruit" for His glory.

- *Lawrence Kimbrough* was responsible for the first round of editing the messages from True Woman '08. His craftsmanship and warm heart have greatly helped to further the mission of Revive Our Hearts.

- *Mike Neises*, Director of Publishing and Events for Revive Our Hearts, has been there each step of the way, navigating, overseeing, and coordinating a myriad of details. He is a stalwart and humble servant *par excellence.*

- My dear friend and regular contributor to the True Woman blog, *Kimberly Wagner*, wrote the first draft of the study guide ("Going Deeper"). She has a passion for the glory of God to be displayed through the lives of Christian women.

• My colaborers on the *Revive Our Hearts team* give of themselves in countless ways to help call women to freedom, fullness, and fruitfulness in Christ. Every undertaking that bears my name, including this book, is enhanced by their faithful efforts on multiple fronts. Special thanks to *Monica Vaught*, who has served as Coordinator for the True Woman conferences. No one has carried the burden and banner for the True Woman movement more earnestly than she.

# Notes

**Front Matter**
1. Susan Hunt, *By Design: God's Distinctive Calling for Women* (Wheaton, IL: Crossway, 1994), 17.

**Part One: Foundations of True Womanhood**
1. Elisabeth Elliot, *Let Me Be a Woman* (Wheaton, IL: Living Books/Tyndale, 1985), epigraph.

**Chapter 1: The Ultimate Meaning of True Womanhood**
1. Karl Olsson, *Passion* (New York: Harper and Row Publishers, 1963), 116–117; also: "Marie Durand Released at Last," Glimpses of Christian History, http://www.chinstitute.org/DAI-LYF/2002/12/daily-12-26-2002.shtml.

2. Randy Alcorn, "The World Was Not Worthy of Them," http://www.epm.org/artman2/publish/persecuted_church/The_World_Was_Not_Worthy_of_Them_Martyrs_for_Christ.shtml.

3. Tim Stafford, "A Heaven-Made Activist," *Christianity Today*, January 2004, 50.

**Chapter 2: From Him, through Him, to Him**
1. http://www.miningreview.com/archive/mra_5_2005/pdf/48-49.pdf.

**Part Two: The Battle for True Womanhood**
1. Cited in John Angell James, *Female Piety: A Young Woman's Friend and Guide* (Morgan, PA: Soli Deo Gloria Publications, 1995), 72.

**Chapter 3: You've Come a Long Way, Baby!**
1. Betty Friedan, *The Feminine Mystique: 20th Anniversary Edition* (New York: Dell Publishing Co., Inc., 1983), 362.

2. http://womenshistory.about.com/od/quotes/a/de_beauvoir_2.htm.

3. Endorsement on back cover of Betty Friedan, *The Feminine Mystique: 20th Anniversary Edition* (New York: Dell Publishing Co., Inc., 1983).

4. Kate Millett, *Sexual Politics* (New York: Random House, 1969), 34.

5. Cited in Marcia Cohan, *The Sisterhood: The Inside Story of the Women's Movement and the Leaders Who Made It Happen* (New York: Ballantine Books, 1988), 286.

6. Cited by Marilyn J. Boxer, "For and About Women: The Theory and Practice of Women's Studies in the United States," in *Feminist Theory: A Critique of Ideology*, eds. Nannerl O. Keohane, Michelle Z. Rosaldo, and Barbara C. Gelpi (Chicago: University of Chicago Press, 1982), 237.

**Part Three: The Refining of True Womanhood**
1. Elisabeth Elliot, *Let Me Be a Woman* (Wheaton, IL: Living Books/Tyndale, 1985), 52.

**Part Four: Reclaiming True Womanhood**
1. John Angell James, *Female Piety: A Young Woman's Friend and Guide* (Morgan, PA: Soli Deo Gloria Publications, 1995), 72–73.

**Chapter 7: God's Jewels**
1. "When He Cometh," words by William O. Cushing (1823–1902).

**Chapter 8: Leaving a Lasting Legacy Through Prayer**
1. Rosalind Rinker, *Prayer: Conversing With God* (Grand Rapids, MI: Zondervan Publishing House, 1959), 23.

2. E. M. Bounds, *Purpose in Prayer* (Grand Rapids, MI: Baker Book House, 1978), 9.

**Chapter 9: A Call to the Counter-Revolution**
1. Norman Grubb, *C. T. Studd: Cricketer & Pioneer* (Fort Washington, PA: Christian Literature Crusade, 2008), 144.